LAKE TAHOE

HOW TO USE THIS GUIDEBOOK

This guidebook is divided into four sections: *An Introduction to Lake Tahoe*, *The History of Lake Tahoe*, *South Lake Tahoe*, and *North Lake Tahoe*.

The first two sections comprise essays, designed to provide you with facts on the area.

In the next two sections we explore the Lake Tahoe Basin, with a detailed, geographical breakdown of the area. Each section contains descriptions of the various places and points of interest, followed by a sub-section entitled *Practical Information*. The *Practical Information* is designed to provide you with a ready reference to accommodations, restaurants, tours, places of interest, recreation areas, transportation, etc., with addresses and phone numbers.

A quick and easy way into this book is the *Index* at the end.

Titles in this Series

Indian Chief Travel Guides are available from your local bookstore or Indian Chief Publishing House, P.O. Box 5205, Tahoe City, CA 95730.

The Complete
LAKE TAHOE
Guidebook

Published by Indian Chief Publishing House
Tahoe City, California

Area Editor: **BALJEET SANGWAN**
Editorial Associate: **PHILLIPPA J. SAVAGE**
Photographs : **Heavenly Valley Ski Resort,
   Northstar-at-Tahoe, B. Sangwan,
   M.S. Dixie Cruises**

ISBN 0-916841-08-1

Printed in the U.S.A.

CONTENTS

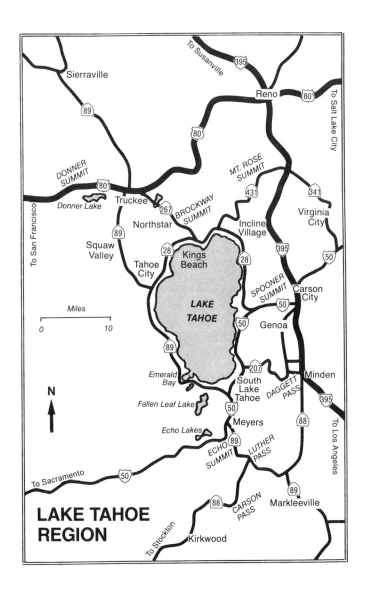

Sierraville

To Susanville

To Salt Lake City

Reno

DONNER SUMMIT

MT. ROSE SUMMIT

Donner Lake

Truckee

BROCKWAY SUMMIT

Incline Village

Virginia City

To San Francisco

Northstar

Squaw Valley

Tahoe City

Kings Beach

LAKE TAHOE

SPOONER SUMMIT

Carson City

Miles

0   10

Genoa

Emerald Bay

South Lake Tahoe

DAGGETT PASS

Minden

N

Fallen Leaf Lake

Echo Lakes

Meyers

To Los Angeles

ECHO SUMMIT

LUTHER PASS

To Sacramento

To Stockton

CARSON PASS

Markleeville

LAKE TAHOE REGION

Kirkwood

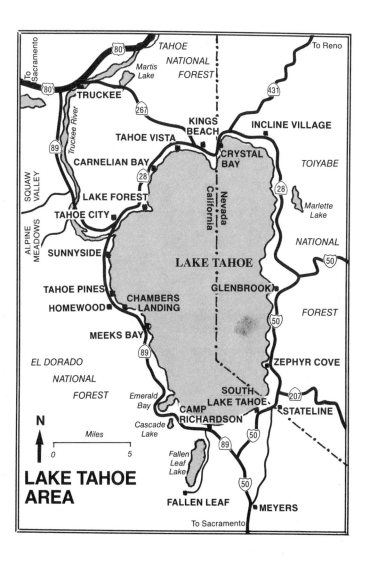

To Sacramento

TAHOE NATIONAL FOREST

To Reno

Martis Lake

80

80

267

431

TRUCKEE

KINGS BEACH

INCLINE VILLAGE

TAHOE VISTA

CRYSTAL BAY

89

CARNELIAN BAY

TOIYABE

Truckee River

28

28

LAKE FOREST

Marlette Lake

SQUAW VALLEY

TAHOE CITY

Nevada
California

NATIONAL

ALPINE MEADOWS

SUNNYSIDE

LAKE TAHOE

50

TAHOE PINES

GLENBROOK

HOMEWOOD

CHAMBERS LANDING

FOREST

50

MEEKS BAY

89

EL DORADO NATIONAL FOREST

ZEPHYR COVE

207

Emerald Bay

SOUTH LAKE TAHOE

STATELINE

N

Cascade Lake

CAMP RICHARDSON

Miles

0   5

Fallen Leaf Lake

89

50

LAKE TAHOE AREA

FALLEN LEAF

50

MEYERS

To Sacramento

7

AN INTRODUCTION TO LAKE TAHOE

A Destination Resort

Lake Tahoe is one of the most beautiful lakes in the world, and the largest among North America's alpine lakes (second largest in the world). Mark Twain once wrote of it: "A noble sheet of blue water lifted six thousand three hundred feet above the level of the sea, and walled in by a rim of snow clad mountain peaks . . . as it lay there with the shadows of the mountains brilliantly photographed upon its still surface, I thought it must surely be the fairest picture the whole earth affords."

Lake Tahoe is situated at an elevation of 6229 feet, more or less in the center of the Sierra Nevada mountain range, with a third of it lying in the State of Nevada and two-thirds in California. From San Francisco the lake is 193 miles distant, and from Reno, Nevada, 54 miles. The lake itself is 22 miles long and 12 miles wide, with a maximum depth of 1645 feet. It is fed by 70 different feeder creeks, streams and rivers, and has a water capacity of 122,160,280 acre-feet (nearly four times that of Lake Mead, the largest man-made lake in the world). Its shoreline measures 71 miles, 42 miles of which lie in California. The Lake Tahoe Basin comprises about 480 square miles (an area larger than Rhode Island), made up mostly of lush, evergreen forests and sculpted granite mountains.

Nearly 11 million people visit the Lake Tahoe (and Reno) area every year, and most come back a second time. There are approximately 10,000 motel rooms and over 200 restaurants to be found in the Tahoe area alone, with hundreds of thousands of acres of preserved wilderness and a vast array of year-round recreational facilities, including fishing, boating, swimming, wind-surfing, hiking, rock-climbing, horseback riding, golf, bicycling and skiing. Lake Tahoe also boasts one of the finest casino districts in the country, with Las Vegas style casinos, and has the largest concentration of ski areas in the world — some 20 different alpine ski resorts, with a total of more than 163 mechanical ski lifts. And to add to this, Lake Tahoe enjoys four distinct seasons: spring, summer, fall and winter. Average snowfall in the region is 300 inches, and yet there are some 250 clear, sunny days every year.

Indeed, Lake Tahoe is among the choicest destination resorts in the world.

THE HISTORY OF
LAKE TAHOE

Lake Tahoe began forming nearly 25 million years ago when portions of the upthrust that comprised the Sierra Nevada mountain range experienced a vast disturbance, causing it to crack and leave a twin, serrated crest and a trough-like depression. More than 20 million years later came the volcanic age, during which huge quantities of lava poured into the trough, pushing masses of boulder ahead of it to form a lateral ridge damming up the southern half of the trough. Then, eight or nine thousand years ago, a massive glacier originating in the south moved northward through the region. This was known as the Lake Valley glacier. Several feeder glaciers from it gouged out the surrounding smaller troughs and valleys. Three fine examples of these are Fallen Leaf Lake, Cascade Lake and Emerald Bay; the Emerald Bay glacier pack actually extended into the oval of Lake Tahoe and later joined the main body of ice. When the ice finally melted, the waters rose several hundred feet above the present level of the lake and forged an outlet in the northwest, through what is now the Truckee River Canyon; although a disputed theory maintains that the Truckee River Canyon was formed by an off-shoot glacier, while the main body of ice moved northeast into Nevada's desert valleys.

Another, less likely version of the formation of Lake Tahoe is offered by an ancient Indian legend, which suggests that Lake Tahoe and all the other smaller lakes and ponds in the region were formed by the mythical "Water Babies," small gray creatures with long dark hair, who have the power to flood the world. It is told that once the Damalalii, a short-tailed weasel, scalped a water baby, and the water baby became angry and flooded the entire region, forcing the Damalalii to return the scalp, lest he drown in the high, rising waters. After the return of the scalp, the waters receded to their present level. And thus was formed Lake Tahoe.

The first known inhabitants of the Lake Tahoe Basin were the Washoe Indians, a mobile people from the arid country east of the Sierra. The Washoe were primarily gathers, with seeds and pinyon nuts comprising their staple diet. In summer they made camp at Lake Tahoe, and fished in its waters. They called the lake "Tahoe," meaning "big water in high place." Others inhabiting the area were the Paiute Indians, who remained largely in the southern parts of the basin. Three larger Indian tribes dwelled in the western foothills of the Sierra, though these never extended their range to Tahoe.

White man first sighted the Sierra Nevada mountain range in 1776: a Franciscan missionary named Pedro Font, member of the Anza expedition, stood on a hill near the mouth of the Sacramento River to behold what he later described as "*un gran sierra nevada*," meaning "a great snow-covered mountain range." But Lake Tahoe was not discovered until nearly seventy years later, on February 14, 1844. The discovery was made by the Fremont Party, led by Captain John Charles Fremont of the U.S. Topographical Engineers, and including Kit Carson, the famous scout, and a German topographer named Charles Preuss. The party was on the eastern ridges of the Sierra, in search of a pass leading from the Carson Valley to the Valley of the Sacramento, when Fremont and Preuss went on ahead to take observations. They ascended what is now known as Red Lake Peak, and saw before them, some 15 miles distant, a vast blue lake, so completely surrounded by mountains that, as Fremont later wrote, they "could not discover an outlet." Fremont named the lake "Bonpland," after the eminent French botanist, Aime Jacques Alexandre Bonpland, who accompanied Barron von Humboldt to explore the west. Preuss made mention of it as the "Mountain Lake." In 1852, however, the lake was named "Bigler," in honor of the Governor of California, John Bigler, who led a rescue party to the aid of a group of emigrants snowbound in Lake Valley that year. But the governor soon fell into disfavor due to his Confederate sympathies during the Civil War, and the lake was renamed in 1861. The lake was then called "Tahoe," after much debate over the precise meaning of the word.

The 1840's, after the discovery, were a period of trailblazing. Several emigrant parties searched for passes over the Sierra range in their attempts to reach the West. The Donner Party is well remembered as part of the region's history. In the winter of 1846-47 the emigrant party led by George Donner became trapped in the treacherous snows near the Donner Pass. They camped just east of the pass, some by the Donner Lake. But the Donner families were ill-prepared for the bitter conditions they encountered, and food soon ran out. Hunger and cold gripped the camp. Several members of the party perished, while the survivors resorted to cannibalism to stay alive until they were found by a rescue party the following spring. Of a party of 89, 42 perished.

With the discovery of gold in 1848, a fresh wave of emigrants and gold seekers swarmed over the Sierra mountains. Several passes were opened up: Lassen, Beckwourth, Carson and Donner. The most traveled route, however, remained by way of Truckee, along which the railroad and Interstate 80 now pass.

In 1851 Lake Tahoe received its first white settler, Martin Smith, who established a trading post in the area known as Meyers now. Others soon followed. A trail was cut through Lake Valley (South Lake Tahoe) the following year by John Calhoun "Cockeye" Johnson, a Sierra pioneer, and appropriately named the Johnson Pass Cut-Off. The route followed roughly the path of present day Highway 50 from Placerville to Lake Valley, descending nearby the Meyers Grade into the valley; then circling around the southern parts of the lake and up along the southeast corner, it passed over the Spooner Summit and into the Carson Valley. In 1896 this became California's first state highway.

The Tahoe basin was mostly wilderness country during the early years, largely inaccessible. But in 1859, the discovery of the Comstock Lode, the richest silver deposit known to history, brought waves of miners and prospectors through Lake Valley enroute to the Washoe mines. In a matter of months the road from Placerville to Carson (City), via Lake Valley, which was essentially the Johnson Pass Cut-off route, became the most traveled in the continent. For nearly a decade wagon trains rolled along this narrow, dusty, rutted trail, almost ceaselessly. In 1860, some 400 wagons traveled this road daily, and more than $1,350,000 was collected in tolls alone. By 1862 the passenger traffic on the road had soared to a staggering 56,500. Over 100 waystations, hotels and saloons sprouted between Placerville and Carson, along what by then had come to be known as the Great Bonanza Road to Washoe, with at least a score and some dotting the Lake Valley section of the road. It is told that many of the waystations collected upwards of $1,000 in tolls in the course of a day, while some of the better saloons raked in as much as $3,000 in a single night. Such were the Bonanza days, a memorable chapter in Lake Valley's past.

Meanwhile, a transcontinental railroad was in the making, largely an endeavor of the Big Four: Charles Crocker, Collis P. Huntington, Mark Hopkins, and Leland Stanford, the Governor of California. Laying of the rails over the Sierra was the hardest part of it. Fifteen tunnels had to be blasted through the granite mountains, and more than 40 miles of track had to be put under cover, building "snow-sheds," to ward off the snow drifts that had hampered work on the tracks. More than 10,000 Chinese were brought in from San Francisco to provide the labor, and a railroad town, now known as Truckee, grew around the work force, just east of the Donner Pass. In April, 1868 the first train crossed the Sierra, eastbound. And the traffic through Lake Valley was diverted to over the Donner Pass.

By the late 1860's silver mining was progressing at a hectic pace just east of the Sierras, with new claims being made and new mines being built, and a burgeoning metropolis growing around it all. This, however, created a new demand: lumber. And Lake Tahoe's virgin forests provided a ready and seemingly inexhaustible source. A half dozen or so logging companies sprouted along the lake's east and south shores. The first shoreline sawmill had been built at Glenbrook in 1861, and now many others began sprouting along the lake's sides. In 1873 the Carson and Tahoe Lumber and Fluming Company was formed by Henry Marvin Yerington and Duane LeRoy Bliss, with Bliss as its president. In the following years the company acquired leases to several thousand acres of timberland, and spawned a vast network of sawmills, flumes, log-chutes, receiving ponds, tug boats, cordwood barges, and even a stretch of railroad employed in the transportation of logs. The company's operations were centered at Glenbrook, on the east shore. But by 1895 the timberlands on the Nevada side were largely depleted; the company had stripped nearly 50,000 acres of forest, leaving behind a scant 950 acres of useable stands of timber, and the operations were then moved to the California side. In its 28 years of operation, the C.& T. L.& F. Company took as much as 750,000,000 board feet of lumber and 500,000 cords of wood from the Lake Tahoe basin.

The late 1890's and early 1900's were good times for Lake Tahoe. Hundreds of summer vacationers thronged the lake's shores, led by social sets from San Francisco and Carson City. The over-water spur tracks and shoreline sawmills of the lumbering days gave way to fastidious over-water clubhouses and luxuriously appointed hostelries. The legendary three and one-half story hotel, The Tallac, billed as "the Saratoga of the Pacific," was built in 1898 on the southwestern shore of the lake. It catered to the well-heeled crowds of the day, providing guests with some of the finest cuisines in the continent, and an array of recreational activities, everything from plain promenading on the pebble beaches to back-packing, horseback riding, swimming, tennis, racquetball and fishing (specially trained guides took guests in fishing boats to the fishing "hot spots" of the lake, practically guaranteeing a catch); and even illegal gambling flourished. The price for lodging alone at The Tallac was $35.00 per week, and up. In 1901, a new "Saratoga," the Tahoe Tavern, was built just south of Tahoe City, and at about the same time a narrow-gauge railroad was pushed through the Truckee River Canyon, from Tahoe City to Truckee, where it linked up with the Southern Pacific.

By the turn of the century the tug boats and cordwood barges of the lumbering days were gone from the scene too, replaced by luxurious steam boats and pleasure vessels, and flotillas of holiday fishing boats. In 1896, the legendary *Tahoe* was launched, a 169-foot, 200-passenger steamer, which ruled the Lake Tahoe waters for some 44 years, until on August 29, 1940, it was scuttled just off the east shore.

The "Roaring 20's" ushered in yet another glorious era, with a host of rambling summer homes appearing quite randomly along the shoreline, among them the fabled "Vikingsholm," the "Thunderbird Lodge," the "Kellogg Mansion," the Pope and Tevis homes at the Tallac Estates, and "Fleur du Lac," industrialist Henry J. Kaiser's vacation home, on the west shore. The 1920's also witnessed the opening up of Tahoe to winter recreation. In fact winter vacationing at the lake was so popular that in 1926 the Southern Pacific introduced its "Snowball" specials to railroad eager tourists from San Francisco to Truckee, and from Truckee to Tahoe City. Just south of Tahoe City, near the Tahoe Tavern, an "Olympic Hill" (comprising a ski jump and a toboggan run) opened up at what became Lake Tahoe's first ski resort — Granlibakken.

In the 1940's, right after World War II, a "casino district" began developing on the south shore, with a handful of casino-clubs cluttering the Nevada side of the stateline. The newly built highway system made travel to Tahoe easier, and the casinos flourished. In 1955 big name entertainment was introduced in Tahoe, mainly the effort of gaming pioneers Eddie Sahati and Harvey Gross, and in 1960 Lake Tahoe's first highrise appeared at the stateline: the 11-story, 200-room Harvey's Resort Hotel.

The year 1960 also brought the VIII Winter Olympic Games to Squaw Valley, 4 miles north of Tahoe City. The games are memorable for one event: the U.S. Hockey Team defeated the Russians 3-2, then went on to defeat Czechoslovakia 9-4 in the finals to win the gold medal. Not until 20 years later, in 1980 at Lake Placid, was the feat repeated.

For the next decade, Lake Tahoe experienced a real estate boom. Property prices soared and hundreds of summer homes sprouted throughout the basin. Large scale development began in the mid-1960's, with condominium complexes appearing along the shoreline. Concern was voiced over the unabated development and the resulting soil erosion, and the impact of it all on the clarity of the lake. The League to Save Lake Tahoe was formed in 1965, comprising mainly wealthy, influential lakers. And in 1969, a bi-state body, the Tahoe Regional Planning Agency, was created, solely for the purpose of controlling and regulating development in the Tahoe basin. New construction in the basin has been severely limited since, and more than 85% of Tahoe's land is now either state or federally owned, creating a bonanza of National Forests and State Parks.

In April of 1982 Lake Tahoe became the focus of the nation. An avalanche at Alpine Meadows leveled the ski lodge and several homes, claiming the lives of seven people. A young ski patrol member, Anna Conrad, miraculously survived the avalanche, buried beneath tons of snow for six whole days and nights.

Once again, in March, 1985, a world event came to Tahoe. Heavenly Valley hosted the prestigious World Cup skiing, and Lake Tahoe was briefly at the center of attention.

Lake Tahoe is today among the choicest destination resorts in the world. But a problem facing it is that of future growth. What direction should this take? How much building should be permitted? What would the environmental impact of it be on the lake? These are questions likely to linger for many years ahead.

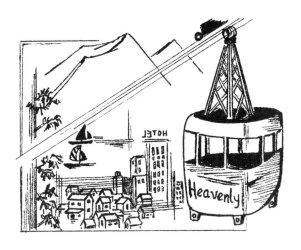

SOUTH LAKE TAHOE

Tahoe's Big Apple

South Lake Tahoe, by Tahoe standards, is a bustling, thriving metropolis, where more than half of the Lake Tahoe Basin's total population lives; roughly 25,000 people. This is also a place that has been largely built around the tourist, with a cluster of highrise hotel-casinos at one end of it, and a federally preserved wilderness at the other. At the center of it lies a lively urban sprawl, concentrated with motels, shops and restaurants — nearly 9000 motel rooms within a space of some 10 square miles, and over 100 restaurants.

The greater South Lake Tahoe comprises broadly five sections: the City of South Lake Tahoe, the Stateline, the Southeast Corner, the Emerald Bay Route area, and the Bonanza Route area. The city is the largest and most central part. To its east lies the (California-Nevada) Stateline, home to South Tahoe's vibrant "casino district," and to its northwest is the Emerald Bay Route, an area of exceptional scenic beauty. South of the city is the historic Bonanza Route, which forms part of the original Great Bonanza Road, path of the "silver seekers" of the 1860's. And the Southeast Corner is the section to the east of the Stateline, comprising eight or nine miles of the southeastern shoreline, and the Kingsbury Grade to the south of there.

South Lake Tahoe can be reached by way of any of three state highways: 50, 89 or (Nevada Route) 207. The Lake Tahoe Airport, Lake Tahoe's only commercial airport, lies just to the south of the city area.

THE BONANZA ROUTE

Highway 50 west is the oldest and most traveled route leading into South Lake Tahoe, having first opened to wagon traffic in the 1850's. From Placerville it winds through several miles of mountain country, through Pollock Pines, Kyburz and Strawberry, following the South Fork of the American River for the most part, then loops over Echo Summit and resolutely descends into Lake Valley (South Lake Tahoe) at the twin divide of the Sierra Nevada-Carson Range. At the foot of the grade, known as the Meyer Grade, one encounters a vast, open meadow in the midst of which sits the township of Meyers, Lake Valley's oldest settlement and now the "gateway" to South Lake Tahoe. Beyond Meyers the highway continues almost directly north, while an historic back road, Pioneer Trail, branches to the northeast just past the township. Pioneer Trail is in fact the original Placerville-Carson back road, upon which much of the Bonanza traffic of the 1860's passed enroute to the Virginia City silver mines. The trail now skirts the City of South Lake Tahoe to the south and merges with the main thoroughfare, Lake Tahoe Boulevard (Highway 50), within two miles of the California-Nevada stateline, where stand South Tahoe's multi-storied hotel-casinos.

This, however, is the Great Bonanza Road, from Placerville to Virginia City, with Pioneer Trail and the Meyers area making up the Lake Tahoe segment of it.

Meyers

Meyers (also known as Tahoe Paradise) is a town of some importance, with a small number of shops and restaurants, two golf courses, a couple of schools, one or two campgrounds, and a rodeo ranch, Amaker's Ranch, which hosts South Tahoe's annual rodeo in summer. Meyers was first settled in 1851 by Martin Smith, Lake Valley's first white settler, though named later on for one George Henry Dudley Meyers, who owned much of the acreage from 1873 until practically the turn of the century. The site of Smith's original trading post, which in 1859 became Yank's Station, named for its illustrious new owner Ephraim "Yank" Clement, is to be seen on the east side of the highway, near the present day Yanks Station Resort; the site is marked by a Pony Express plaque, for Yank's in the 1860's, besides being the most colorful hostelry on the Bonanza Route, was also a remount station for Pony Express riders. Meyers, today, is also noted for its many hiking and nordic ski areas, a favorite among which is the Echo Lakes area, just two miles to the southwest, where a trail enchantingly journeys along the periphery of both the Upper and Lower Echo Lakes. In winter one may even find a snowmobiling meadow or two in the

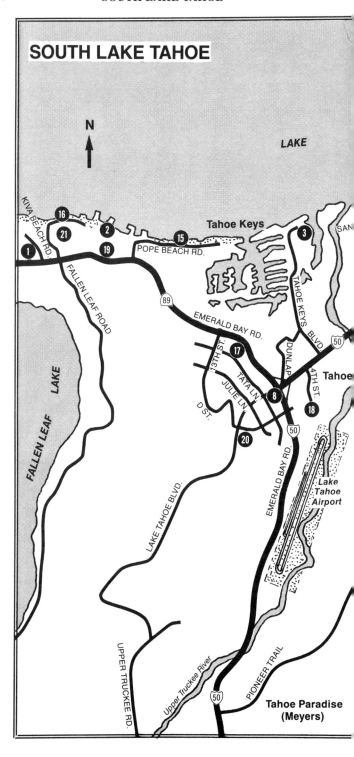

SOUTH LAKE TAHOE

N

LAKE

KIVA BEACH RD.

16

21   2   Tahoe Keys

1   19   15   POPE BEACH RD.   3   SAN

FALLEN LEAF ROAD   TAHOE KEYS BLVD.

89   50

EMERALD BAY RD.

FALLEN LEAF LAKE   1ST ST.   17   DUNLAP   4TH ST.   Tahoe

13TH ST.   TATA LN.   8   18

D ST.   JULIE LN.

20   50

EMERALD BAY RD.   Lake
Tahoe
Airport

LAKE TAHOE BLVD.

UPPER TRUCKEE RD.   Upper Truckee River   50   PIONEER TRAIL   Tahoe Paradise
(Meyers)

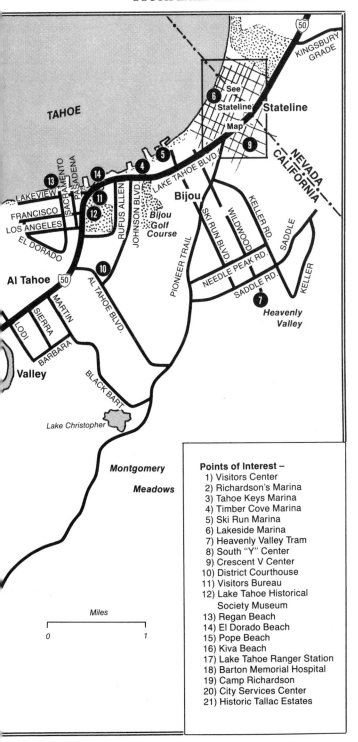

Points of Interest –
1) Visitors Center
2) Richardson's Marina
3) Tahoe Keys Marina
4) Timber Cove Marina
5) Ski Run Marina
6) Lakeside Marina
7) Heavenly Valley Tram
8) South "Y" Center
9) Crescent V Center
10) District Courthouse
11) Visitors Bureau
12) Lake Tahoe Historical
   Society Museum
13) Regan Beach
14) El Dorado Beach
15) Pope Beach
16) Kiva Beach
17) Lake Tahoe Ranger Station
18) Barton Memorial Hospital
19) Camp Richardson
20) City Services Center
21) Historic Tallac Estates

Miles

0   1

vicinity of the town, and a handful of ski rental shops along the highway. Worth visiting too are a couple of local restaurants, including Ristorante Tre Fontane which serves some delightful Italian fare, and the Freel Peak Saloon, a casual, inexpensive diner, named for the mighty Freel Peak, the highest mountain at the lake with an elevation of 10,900 feet, seen farther to the east of here.

Pioneer Trail

Pioneer Trail is a lovely, tree-lined back road, some 7 miles long, frequently used as a city bypass route when traveling directly from Meyers to the Stateline. During the 1860's this was known as the "Placerville-Carson back road," for then, as now, the main road (the lakeshore road) ran farther to the north. The trail is noted mostly for its historic past, in particular the Bonanza era when it became one of the most traveled roads in the continent, with what has been described as "the greatest mass movement of men, wagons, materials, animals and bullion known to history," passing by way of it. A dozen or so waystations and hostelries were then located alongside of the trail, the sites of which have been marked with wooden pegs by the Lake Tahoe Historical Society, and can be visited; not all of these markers are readily visible though, with one or two of them really quite difficult to find, but it is nevertheless a worthwhile pursuit, especially for history buffs. (A guidebook worth taking along when exploring these sites is the Historical Society publication, *Lake Valley's Past,* which details an auto tour of these and other historical sites in the South Tahoe area, with numbered markers to go by.)

The site of Yank's Station, though actually in Meyers now, is considered to be the westernmost of the back road sites, with two others, the sites of the Celio Ranch and Osgood's Toll House, to be found farther southeast at the foot of the Meyers Grade. On the actual trail, however, proceeding northeast one first arrives at the site of Pine Grove House, located on the east side of the trail, one and one-half miles from Yank's. The Pine Grove House was built in 1860, expressly for the Bonanza trade, and by 1888 it was gone from the scene, gutted by fire. It had comprised of one house and one barn.

One-half mile farther, on the same side of the road, is to be found the site of Woodburn's Mill, where Robert Woodburn, a native of Ireland, built one of Lake Tahoe's earliest sawmills, the first ever to be powered by water, in 1860. The 10-horsepower mill churned out a daily quota of 6000 board feet of double-width, out-size lumber, some of which is still to be seen in the sidewalls of one or two of Lake Valley's oldest homes. In its heyday, Woodburn's boasted a handful of logger's cabins, corrals for horses and cattle, a blacksmith's shop and even a post office. But by the late 1800's the lumbering settlement had all but vanished from the scene. One or two pieces of the mill machinery have been salvaged by the Lake Tahoe Historical Society and can be viewed at its museum on Lake Tahoe Boulevard.

At a pebble's throw from Woodburn's, where Trout Creek crosses

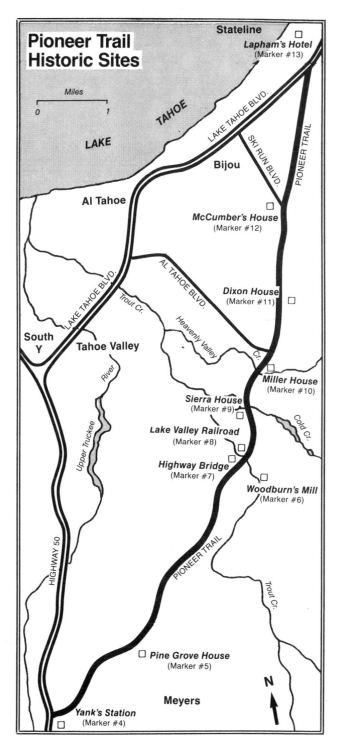

Pioneer Trail Historic Sites

Stateline

Lapham's Hotel
(Marker #13)

Miles

0 1

TAHOE

LAKE

LAKE TAHOE BLVD.

SKI RUN BLVD.

PIONEER TRAIL

Bijou

Al Tahoe

McCumber's House
(Marker #12)

AL TAHOE BLVD.

LAKE TAHOE BLVD.

Trout Cr.

Dixon House
(Marker #11)

Heavenly Valley

South Y

Tahoe Valley

Cr.

Miller House
(Marker #10)

River

Sierra House
(Marker #9)

Cold Cr.

Lake Valley Railroad
(Marker #8)

Upper Truckee

Highway Bridge
(Marker #7)

Woodburn's Mill
(Marker #6)

HIGHWAY 50

PIONEER TRAIL

Trout Cr.

Pine Grove House
(Marker #5)

N

Meyers

Yank's Station
(Marker #4)

21

beneath Pioneer Trail, there is to be found a small bridge from the post-Bonanza era, said to be the first such bridge constructed across the thoroughfare. The bridge is actually located just below the trail, on the west side of it. Above the bridge, just to the north of the creek, is the site of the Lake Valley Railroad tracks; it was along here that during the lumbering days of the 1880's the railroad passed. Impressions of the tracks had been visible for nearly one-half century after the dismantling of the railroad, but are now mostly overgrown with shrubs.

Beyond the bridge and the site of the railroad tracks, also on the west side of the trail, is to be found the site of the most colorful of the back road hostelries: the Sierra House. A two-story log structure with an added saloon, the Sierra House was built in 1859 by Robert Garwood Dean, nephew of Judge Seneca Dean, who later went on to partake in the construction of the Lake Bigler House, the lake's first shoreline hostelry. Legend has it that Black Bart and Jack Bell, the notorious highway robbers, lodged at the Sierra House during the peak of their crime activities, and that "Long Haired" Sam Brown — the coward killer from Washoe who carved 20 notches on the butt of his gun and maintained a private cemetary — as well as James Stewart, the "Silent Terror," frequented the Sierra House saloon. Later, even "The Whipped Murderess of Hangtown," notorious for poisoning her male companions, who was believed to have been whipped across her face by one of her victims, stayed a night here. By 1955, however, the Sierra House, not unlike other structures of the day, had been gutted by fire. Some of the lumber from the hostelry's outbuildings is now to be seen panelling one of the interior walls of the Sierra House School, located nearby.

A little over a mile northeast of the Sierra House site is the site of the Miller Station, a lesser known waystation, built in 1862 by John G. Miller to capitalize on the Washoe trade. And another half-mile from there, on the east side of the trail, is seen the site of Dixon House, an 80 feet long and 38 feet wide log structure, built in 1861. The Dixon House was named for the Dixon family, who owned and operated the hostelry from 1867 until it disappeared from the scene more than 50 years later.

Also on the east side of the road, approximately 200 yards south of Ski Run Boulevard, is the site of McCumber's House, where an early day laker named Freeman McCumber built a large two-story structure, with a domineering stone chimney and five outbuildings, in 1864. McCumber's was originally built as a primary residence but quickly fell prey to the Bonanza trade, and by the mid-1950's, it, too, had disappeared from the back road. The site has since been built upon with a private home.

The last site on the Placerville-Carson back road, located more or less on the "back road Y," is that of Lapham's Hotel, variously known as Lapham's Landing, Stateline Hotel, Carney's Station and Lakeside. Actually, quite like the site of Yank's Station, this site is no longer on Pioneer Trail, for the trail ends at Lake Tahoe Boulevard, and Lapham's lies north of the boulevard at the lake end of Park Avenue, where the present day Lakeside Marina is now to be seen. Lapham's was named for William W. Lapham, who built and owned the hotel from 1860 until 1875, when it finally burned to the ground.

THE CITY

The City of South Lake Tahoe, incorporated on November 30, 1965, is Tahoe's only real city. It covers an area of approximately 26 square miles, taking in the subdivisions of Tahoe Valley, Tahoe Keys, Al Tahoe, Bijou and Lakeside; and it is bounded by the California-Nevada stateline and the El Dorado National Forest on the east and west, respectively, with the world-renowned Heavenly Valley and the Montgomery Meadows to its south and some 6 miles of shoreline to be enjoyed along its north.

If you take Highway 50 directly into South Lake Tahoe, past Meyers and the Pioneer Trail turnoff, the first signs of city life to be encountered are at the South Tahoe Y, where Highways 50 and 89 intersect and where city traffic and traffic signals become a glaring reality. The "Y" more or less represents the western end of the city. From here Highway 50 travels in a northeasterly direction to the Al Tahoe shoreline, then dips slightly before heading directly east to the Stateline, from where it follows a northeasterly course again, past the Kingsbury Grade turnoff. The section of highway between the "Y" and the Kingsbury Grade turnoff is known as Lake Tahoe Boulevard. This is the city's main street, upon which much of the city's activity is centered, with scores of hotels, motels, timeshare condominiums, shops, restaurants and even some wedding chapels to be seen along here. The city also has an in-city campground, a golf course, a modest hospital, a couple of recreation areas, a visitors' information center, a museum and a Chamber of Commerce, all nestled along the boulevard. Most other urban and recreational facilities are to be found on four or five of the other major streets of the city, such as the Rufus Allen and Al Tahoe Boulevards, Park Avenue, Stateline Avenue and Ski Run Boulevard. Thus, in many ways, the city is really quite easy to explore, with little need to deviate from the major thoroughfares.

Tahoe Valley

Tahoe Valley is the westernmost section of the city, bordered on the west and northwest by the El Dorado National Forest and on the east by the Upper Truckee River. At the heart of the valley lies the South Tahoe Y (also known as the Tahoe Valley Y), crossroads of South Lake Tahoe for over a century, and now a vital business center of the valley. At the Y is to be found the South Y Center, one of South Tahoe's two biggest shopping centers, with two chain stores, a splendid bookstore, a movie theatre, and several small novelty stores and fast food outlets. A half-dozen or so smaller shopping squares, including the Lampson Plaza, are located nearby, within a two-mile radius of the Y. Just south of the Y are located two well-patronized campgrounds, and farther south of there the Lake Tahoe Airport, a splendid mountain airport that dates from 1959. The airport, situated at an elevation of 6264 feet, boasts an 8544-foot north-south runway and a lovely shingled terminal building with a domineering A-Frame facade; the terminal was built in 1973. A half-mile or so south of the airport lies the Lake Tahoe Country Club, an 18-hole, 6588-yard golf course that offers some exciting snowmobiling possibilities in winter.

North of the Y, on the Emerald Bay Road section of Highway 89, are seen a couple of rows of rustic motels, interspersed with some excellent restaurants, notable among which are the Chez Villaret, a charming French restaurant, and Cantina Los Tres Hombres, which serves some delightful Mexican fare. Also of interest here is the Cookbook, which boasts "one of the largest omelette menus in the world, with over 500 omelette combinations." During the summer months a couple of bicycle and moped rental outlets can be found along here too.

West of the Y lies a small, relatively quiet part of town, backed by the twin-peaked Tahoe Mountain (elevations 7249 and 7127 feet). Here are to be found a handful of residential tracts, a trailer park or two, and the City Administration and City Services centers, both of which are located on Tata Lane.

To the east of the Y is sprawled a bustling business district, disected quite cleanly by Lake Tahoe Boulevard. About a mile and a half from the Y, just south of the Boulevard, is to be found the Barton Memorial Hospital, the south shore's only full-fledged medical facility, originally built in 1963. And several blocks to the east of there one can visit the Swiss Chalet, an open-ended mall built in the European country tradition, with stucco walls, dark walnut trim and Tudor murals on the feature walls; there are some worthwhile variety stores and a delightful Swiss restaurant housed at the Chalet. Farther along, just past the intersection of Lake Tahoe Boulevard and Tahoe Keys Boulevard, sits the Jewelry Factory, made famous by Liberace and Sammy Davis, Jr., both of whom are said to buy much of their jewelry here. Adjacent to the Jewelry Factory is seen a large native stone building with glass doors, quite characteristic in its bold construction; this houses The Outdoorsman, the lake's largest sporting goods store, where one can buy anything from a simple hiking guidebook to fishing accessories, scuba diving outfits, ski equipment, bicycles, hunting knives and rifles. Not far from The Outdoorsman the Upper Truckee River crosses beneath the highway as it makes for the lake; in spring one can stand on the bridge above the river and watch large schools of whitefish emerge from their spawning beds farther upstream.

Tahoe Keys

Almost directly north of Tahoe Valley lies Tahoe Keys, the smallest, newest, and most affluent section of the city. Tahoe Keys is made up of long narrow, lateral projections of land, with most of the homes here enjoying secluded waterfronts. Of particular interest at the "Keys" is the Tahoe Keys Marina, home port of the *Spirit of Tahoe Keys,* one of the most luxurious charter boats at the lake; several other expensive craft, owned by wealthy sailors and boating enthusiasts, are to be seen moored here as well. The marina is located at the very end of Venice Drive (which runs off the Tahoe Keys Boulevard), and to be also found here, situated on the lake, is the Fresh Ketch, a delightful seafood restaurant.

Just west of Tahoe Keys lies the Truckee Marsh, characterized by scrub and brush and shallow water, and to the east the Upper Truckee River fans out into the lake, with several frolicking rafters to be seen here in the summer, floating into the lake at the end of their river ride.

Al Tahoe

Adjoining Tahoe Keys and Tahoe Valley on the east is Al Tahoe, a section of town that officially came into being in 1907 when a hotel of the same name was built here by one "Al" Sprague, who tacked on his "Al" to "Tahoe" to give the establishment a name. The original Al Tahoe subdivision, a triangular tract with a lake frontage, lies to the northwest of Lake Tahoe Boulevard, just where the boulevard swoops northeast to hug the shoreline. Several old homes and cottages, many of them dating from the 1920's, are to be found dotting the streets here. The site of the original Al Tahoe Hotel can be seen at the corner of Sacramento Street and Lakeview Avenue; upon it there now stands the Globin Home, a fire-brick building with a hand-hewn upper deck that looks out over the lake, originally built in 1924 as part of the old Globin Resort. Four or five well-aged cottages, part of the former Globin Resort, are scattered farther back on Sacramento Street. Just below the Globin Home lies Regan Beach, a lovely stretch of yellow sand, and at the edge of the subdivision, about one-half mile east of the influx of the Upper Truckee River into the lake, is seen the site of Lake House (also known as Lake Bigler House), the first of Lake Tahoe's shoreline hostelries, built in 1859 and gutted by fire in 1866.

Adjacent to the triangular Al Tahoe tract, on the east side of it, are to be found the tiny El Dorado Recreation Area and a thin strip of beach of the same name, both wedged between the highway and the lake; the recreation area features a dozen or so park benches, all looking out over the lake. South of the recreation area, on the other side of the highway, lies the green rectangle of the City Campground, with some 166 campsites, and beside the campground, in a park-like setting is to be found a cluster of small brown buildings, housing the South Lake Tahoe Chamber of Commerce, the Lake Tahoe Arts Center, the South Tahoe Visitors Bureau and the Lake Tahoe Historical Society Museum. The museum is of particular interest, with several displays of old photographs depicting Lake Valley's past to be viewed within, as well as some interesting artifacts, a few of them of Indian origin. An out-sized bobsled dating from the 1920's is also to be viewed here, with some 19th century farm machinery to be seen just outside the museum building. Directly across the street from the complex sits the gray and white Tribune Building, home to the *Tahoe Daily Tribune*, Lake Tahoe's only daily newspaper.

The City Campground is flanked on its east by the Rufus Allen Boulevard, where one can visit the new City Library, with its many volumes of books providing for some literary interest. Nearby, roughly at the corner of Rufus Allen and the highway, is seen a weathered, dark-brown cabin, 40 feet square and propped on pilings. This is the

Osgood Toll House, the lake's oldest structure, originally built in 1859 by one Nehemiah Osgood, and located at the foot of the Meyers Grade. It was then a colorful Bonanza Route waystation, and also the site of an historic shootout between two highway robbers and the sheriff and his posse. The toll house was moved to its present location in the early 1970's.

Also of interest at Al Tahoe are the half-dozen or so wedding chapels, each quite charming in its own way. Other points of interest here include the South Lake Tahoe Presbyterian Church, a rambling stone structure, and the rustic American Legion Building; both are located on Lake Tahoe Boulevard, almost directly across from one another. Also, at the corner of Johnson and Al Tahoe Boulevards are to be found the County Administration Building and the Judicial Courts, two fine examples of modern Tahoe architecture, featuring extensive use of native stone. The Judicial Courts Building is especially interesting with its great stone pillars and recessed second floor windows. There are some wonderfully landscaped grounds here too, shaded with several splendid trees.

Bijou

Bijou (meaning "gem" or "jewel") is the easternmost section of the city, named for a beautiful granite sand beach that once graced its shoreline, until in 1910 the damming of the lake's only outlet at Tahoe City and the subsequent raising of the lake level devoured it completely. Bijou is the south shore's oldest business center, where in the 1880's and 1890's much of Lake Valley's large scale lumbering operations were centered. It has since grown into one of the most intensely developed sections of the city, with a wealth of fine shops, restaurants and motels, quite like any vibrant city center. Several sections of Bijou are well worth exploring on foot, though mostly at random, with special emphasis on the section between Ski Run Boulevard and Park Avenue, where the development is almost uninterrupted. There are a handful of quite exclusive timeshare condominium complexes to be found in the area as well, notable among which is the Beach and Ski Club.

Bijou also has two delightful marinas, the Timber Cove Marina and the Ski Run Marina. Timber Cove is the older of the two, located just to the back of the Timber Cove Lodge, and not readily visible from the highway. It is noted for its 1000-foot pier, which is among the longest at the lake. Just to the west of the Timber Cove pier is seen the site of the ancient Bijou Pier, which was said to have measured some 1800 feet, with the Lake Valley Railroad's narrow-gauge tracks running onto it, all the way to the far end; it was from here that Lake Valley's lumber was barged across the lake to the Glenbrook sawmills on the east shore during the lumbering days of the late 1800's. To the east of the Timber Cove Marina, situated at the foot of Ski Run Boulevard, is the Ski Run Marina, home port of the majestic *Tahoe Queen*, a 500-passenger, glass-bottomed cruise boat built in the Mississippi riverboat tradition, with a giant red paddlewheel mounted on its stern, white lace trim and rails along its open deck and passageways, and two great black chimneys rising above. The *Queen* cruises the lake waters year-round, featuring some worthwhile Emerald Bay Cruises, and Squaw Valley shuttles to the north shore in winter. South from the marina Ski Run Boulevard heads toward the world famous Heavenly Valley, with an array of ski rental shops to be seen dotting the roadsides enroute, interspersed with one or two hot-tub rental houses, including Shingle Creek Hot Tubs and Nephele's.

Also of interest at Bijou is the Bijou Golf Course, a 9-hole, 2015-yard course located between Fairway Avenue and Johnson Boulevard, just off the highway. This is the only in-city golf course, open to the public in summer.

To the east of Bijou lies Lakeside, a robust little section of town, with its own marina, shopping district and motel blocks; and adjoining to the east of there is the (California-Nevada) Stateline.

STATELINE

The Stateline is one of the most vibrant parts of South Lake Tahoe and in many ways the hub of the area, with at least four different routes — Highway 50 west, Highway 50 east, the Kingsbury Grade (Nevada Route 207) and Pioneer Trail — converging in on it. On the Nevada side of it lies the celebrated "casino district" of South Tahoe, where stand some of the lake's finest hotel-casinos, and on the California side is seen a profusion of motels and specialty shops, with most of these referring to their location as being "at the Stateline." And farther south from the casinos and motels lies Heavenly Valley, "America's largest alpine ski resort," part of it in Nevada and part in California.

Thus, in a rather broad, informal sort of way, the greater "Stateline" takes in the casino district, the small, ill-defined tract on the California side which theoretically belongs with the City of South Lake Tahoe, and, for practical purposes, even Heavenly Valley — (although in a stricter sense the "Stateline" is only a small postal district on the Nevada side of the border).

The Casino District

Central to the Stateline is, of course, the casino district, a quarter-square-mile tract extending from the stateline east to Edgewood, along which are nestled a group of 24-hour casino-clubs and some of Tahoe's tallest buildings, fourteen, fifteen and eighteen stories high. For visitors to the area the district is a must. Here is to be found some of the most thrilling, non-stop gambling action — with a variety that ranges from slot machines to craps, keno, blackjack, roulette and even betting on horse races and ball games — and star-studded live entertainment. At virtually any hour of the day or night, one can see casino-goers bobbing along the sidewalks here, stalking in and out of clubs, courtesy buses darting back and forth between the clubs and the motels, tour

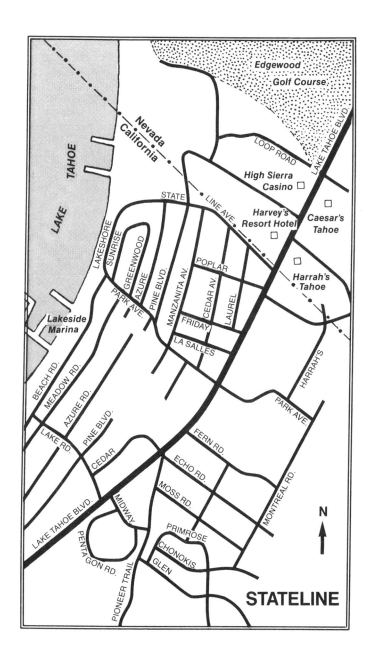

Edgewood
Golf Course

Nevada
California

LAKE TAHOE

LOOP ROAD

LAKE TAHOE BLVD.

High Sierra
Casino

STATE

LINE AVE.

Harvey's
Resort Hotel

Caesar's
Tahoe

LAKESHORE

SUNRISE

GREENWOOD

AZURE

PINE BLVD.

PARK AVE.

MANZANITA AV.

POPLAR

CEDAR AV.

LAUREL

Harrah's
Tahoe

Lakeside
Marina

FRIDAY

LA SALLES

HARRAH'S

BEACH RD.

MEADOW RD.

AZURE RD.

PINE BLVD.

PARK AVE.

LAKE RD.

CEDAR

FERN RD.

ECHO RD.

MONTREAL RD.

LAKE TAHOE BLVD.

MIDWAY

MOSS RD.

PENTAGON RD.

PRIMROSE

CHONOKIS

GLEN

PIONEER TRAIL

N

STATELINE

buses giving out-of-area residents a preview of the district, and yellow cabs preying for fares at the casino-entrances. You can walk beneath marquees featuring some of the biggest and most glamorous names in the entertainment world, and feast on some of the finest gourmet foods as well as 99¢ ham and eggs breakfasts. Most of the shows, too, are moderately priced, and well worth it.

There are five hotel-casinos to be found in the district — Harrah's Tahoe, Harvey's Resort Hotel, Caesar's Tahoe, the High Sierra and Barney's — with two others, Lakeside Inn & Casino and John's Tahoe Nugget, lying just outside the district at the foot of the Kingsbury Grade. Oldest on the block is Harvey's, propped right up at the state-line with barely inches to spare between its west wall and the State of California (where gambling, as practiced in Reno and Las Vegas, is illegal). Harvey's has actually grown out of an early day gambling establishment of sorts, the Wagon Wheel Saloon, which appeared on the scene, upon this very site, in 1946, opening for business with a six-stool counter, three slot machines, two pool tables, and a 24-hour gas pump to lure the occasional motorist. In 1960, gaming pioneer Harvey Gross, for whom the casino is named, built the present-day 11-story, 200-room resort hotel which, most notably, became Lake Tahoe's first highrise. More recently, however, the addition of a new 22-story, 547-room wing to the original hotel has given Harvey's yet another distinction — it is now the tallest building at the lake. Worth visiting at Harvey's is the Top of the Wheel restaurant and lounge which offers unparalleled, panoramic views of the lake and the Sierras. Also of interest at the hotel is a glass elevator which, again, offers some great views of the lake as it climbs from the casino floor to the Top of the Wheel.

Directly across the street from Harvey's is the Harrah's Tahoe Hotel-Casino, with its out-size parking lot spilling over into the California side, offering a unique opportunity for driving into the club through one state and leaving via another. Harrah's is 18 stories high, built in 1973 by Bill Harrah, who in the late 1950's, after building the Harrah's Reno Hotel, was glamorized as "the biggest gambler in the world," until Howard Hughes went on his historic buying spree in Las Vegas in the mid-1960's and wrested the title. The hotel boasts 540 well-appointed guest rooms and over 70,000 square feet of casino space. Of particular interest at Harrah's is The Summit lounge and restaurant, from where spectacular, all-round views of Lake Tahoe can be enjoyed.

Adjoining the Harrah's hotel on the east is the Harrah's Sports-book, a tiny extension of the main building, which caters to betting on horse races and ball games. And to the east of there is Barney's, the smallest club on the block.

Farther east from Harrah's and Barney's is to be found the glamorous Caesar's Tahoe, part of the Caesar's Palace, Las Vegas chain. Caesar's is a 15-story hotel with a worthwhile shopping arcade and one or two delightful restaurants, including Edgewood which is billed as "one of the most elegant restaurants in Northern Nevada." Across the street from Caesar's stands the 14-story High Sierra Hotel-Casino, formerly known as the Sahara, built in 1965. It features an "Old West" decor, and a warm, friendly atmosphere, with even the employees sporting cowboy hats and waistcoats. A place of interest here is Lily's, where nightly dancing can be enjoyed.

East of the casino district are to be found the two "outlying" clubs, Lake Tahoe Inn and John's Tahoe Nugget, both relatively small but with considerable enthusiasm for gambling and live entertainment.

The California Side

The California side of the Stateline, especially the section between Stateline Avenue and Park Avenue, is among the most densely populated parts of South Lake Tahoe, best explored on foot. The Lake Tahoe Boulevard runs through the midst of here, as elsewhere in the city, and alongside of it are seen several specialty shops, most of them peddling "Tahoe" souvenirs in every shape, size and color. Three or four well-equipped sporting goods stores are to be found along here too, including The Outdoorsman ski shop, the Mountain Granite Shop and the Sugar House; and a handful of restaurants, with one or two of them located on the highway, are worth visiting as well. During the hectic summer season one can even find tiny "information" booths dotting the sidewalks along here, freely dispensing timeshare condominium literature. North of Lake Tahoe Boulevard, down to Lakeside Avenue, is "motel country," where scores of motels, all vying for the tourist trade beneath bright-eyed "vacancy" signs, stand shoulder to shoulder on the half-dozen or so little streets criss-crossing through there. South of the boulevard on Park Avenue lies the Crescent V Center, one of South Tahoe's two biggest shopping centers, and at the lake end of Park Avenue is located the Lakeside Marina, a favorite with summer vacationers, from where one can take cruises to beautiful Emerald Bay on board the *Miss Tahoe*. During the 1860's and 1870's, Lakeside was the site of Lapham's Hotel and Landing, and the stateline was thought to run through the center of it; but four decades and four surveys later, the stateline was established some 2000 feet to the northeast. Lakeside, until nearly the turn of the century, was also the scene of Washoe Indian love feasts, or fandangos.

Heavenly Valley

Heavenly Valley is a place of superlatives: it is America's largest alpine ski resort; it has the highest skiable point at the lake, atop Monument Peak, elevation 10,100 feet; and it boasts one of the steepest ski trails in America, the Motts Canyon Trail, located in Heavenly North on the Nevada side. Heavenly is also, in some ways, the playground of the rich and the famous: every year in February it hosts the John Denver Celebrity Ski Classic, to which flock some of Hollywood's most illustrious stars, and in March, 1985, it even hosted the World Cup skiing, one of the most prestigious ski events.

The ski resort is actually sprawled over nine different mountains and more than 20 square miles of forest land, much of it leased from the U.S. Forest Service. It is unique in that a third of it lies in California and two-thirds in Nevada, with a ski trail leading over the top of it, enabling one to ski from one state into the other. There are three base lodges here — the California Base Lodge, and Stagecoach and

Boulder — and a handful of day lodges perched at higher elevations. Heavenly also boasts over 100 ski runs, the oldest of which, Gunbarrel, originally opened to skiers in December 1955; and there are some 26 mechanical lifts here to carry skiers to the tops of the mountains. Of particular interest at Heavenly, however, is the aerial tram, which takes one from the California Base Lodge to the delightful Top of the Tram restaurant some 2000 feet above lake level, with splendid, panoramic views of the lake and the surrounding mountains to be enjoyed enroute. Interestingly, the 50-passenger tram cars travel along a cable length of 1400 feet to achieve a vertical rise of 1700 feet. The tram ride takes 3 minutes and 38 seconds to the top.

Also to be found on the California side, just below the ski resort, are some excellent lodging facilities, including the Heavenly Valley Townhouses, and the greatly talked about Christiania Inn, a charming, alpine inn and restaurant, noted for its warmth and creative desserts. A half-dozen or so ski shops are to be found around here too, mainly on Ski Run Boulevard on the way to the Heavenly slopes, and located at the top of the boulevard is a commercial sled hill, complete with saucer rentals and even accommodations, known as Hansen's Resort.

On the Nevada side, near the base lodges, are seen some interesting mountain homes and condominiums, especially striking along the approaches to the Stagecoach Lodge, where most of them look out over the Carson Valley. Approaches to the Stagecoach and Boulder lodges are via Quaking Aspen Lane and Benjamin Drive, respectively.

THE SOUTHEAST CORNER

The southeast corner of the lake, quite in contrast to the dazzling Stateline and the equally vibrant city area, is made up of a dozen or so tiny, independent, and more or less rural communities, among them Edgewood, Round Hill, Zephyr Cove, Cave Rock, Logan Shoals, Glenbrook and Kingsbury. An attempt to explore these, however, involves two separate excursions: one north along the shoreline; the other east over the Kingsbury Grade.

Kingsbury Grade

The Kingsbury Grade is just to the southeast of the Stateline casinos, off Highway 50. It is noted for its spectacular drive which takes the motorist on a steep ascent to the Daggett Summit (elevation 7375 feet), then in a dramatic plunge down the Haines Canyon and into the Carson Valley, a descent of some 3000 feet being achieved in just over 6 miles. Along the way a great deal of scenery presents itself, with a Lookout Point being reached about halfway down the mountain, from where views of the Carson Valley and its green rectangles of farmland dotted with tiny brown farm-houses, is breathtaking. The grade also has some historic merit. The travel route over the grade was first built in 1860 as part of the original Overland Pony Express Route, and named for its builder, David Demmen Kingsbury. In fact, this is the historic Kingsbury-Daggett Pass Cut-off over which the Bonanza traffic of the 1860's passed. At the bottom of the grade, just to the south are now to be found the twin townships of Minden and Gardnerville, the latter being noted for its excellent Basque restaurants, and the much-talked-about Walley's Hot Springs Resort, which dates from 1862. Just to the north of the foot of the grade lies Genoa, Nevada's oldest settlement, where a group of Mormons established a trading post in 1849. At Genoa one can now visit gaming pioneer Harvey Gross' ranch, famous for its herds of bison.

On the west face of the grade, just above the Highway 50 turnoff and overlooking the lake, is nestled the Kingsbury Village, a small but robust community with a host of small shopping squares, some good restaurants, bowling lanes, two banking companies, a medical clinic, a school and a post office. Adjacent to the Kingsbury Village lies the Tahoe Village, another small, interesting community, though primarily residential; some fascinating mountain construction is to be seen at the eastern end of the village, with homes and condominiums fearlessly perched on the edge of the mountain, overlooking the Carson Valley thousands of feet below. Several splendid resort developments, such as the Tahoe Sierra Resort and the Tahoe Seasons Resort, are to be found here too. Heavenly Valley North adjoins just to the back of Tahoe Village, reached via Benjamin Drive.

Edgewood to Zephyr Cove

Northeast of the Stateline lies Edgewood, not an essentially populous community, but with a golf course of considerable interest. The Edgewood Golf Course, rated by *Golf Digest* as one of the top ten public courses in the country, is an 18-hole, 7563-yard championship course with three-quarters of a mile of beach frontage, accessible from Loop Road, south of which stands the High Sierra Hotel-Casino.

Directly across from the Edgewood Golf Course, situated in an open meadow on the east side of the highway, is the historic Friday's Station, a charming, Bonanza era hostelry, characteristic in its hand-hewn posts and rails, originally built in 1860 by one "Friday" Burke, for whom it is named. In the 1860's this was also a Pony Express stop, with "Pony Bob" Haslem, one of the most celebrated Pony Express riders, headquartered here. The hostelry is now a private home, beautifully restored by its owners. It can be viewed from the highway, or Loop Road.

It is approximately one and one-half miles from Edgewood to Round Hill (also known as Round Mound), where a well-rounded knoll, some 500 feet above lake level, can be seen on the west side of the highway. Round Hill has a noteworthy shopping mall with several interesting shops and one or two fine dining and entertainment establishments, including Zachary's which is a worthwhile steakhouse, and the After Dark nightclub, excellent for all night dancing and entertainment. Below the Round Mound lies the Nevada Beach, a lovely stretch of yellow sand with some picnicking possibilities, and to the

Heavenly Valley's aerial tram offers panoramic views of the lake

Emerald Bay, Lake Tahoe

east is Elk Point, a tiny bit of land jutting out into the lake.

Above Elk Point one finds the small, secluded Marla Bay, its contour vaguely resembling the profile of an Indian. The northern corner of the bay is described by a large, horn-like land mass known as Zephyr Point, which further, to its north, encloses a lovely crescent-chaped cove of the same name: Zephyr Cove. Although named for the strong afternoon winds that sometimes sweep across it from the Emerald Bay gorge and the Rubicon Range in the west, Zephyr Cove is a remarkably beautiful, self-contained summer resort. Besides having a delightful sandy beach and a marina, it is also the home port of the *M.S. Dixie*, Lake Tahoe's oldest cruise boat in service, which made its debut on the lake in 1947. The *Dixie,* much like the *Tahoe Queen,* is a glass-bottomed Mississippi river-boat, quite spectacular with its giant red paddlewheel propelling it across the lake. A variety of cruises can be taken on board it, including ones to beautiful Emerald Bay. Also berthed at the cove is a large trimaran known as the *Woodwind,* said to be the largest sailing vessel at the lake; some memorable cruises can be enjoyed on board this, sailing quite randomly into the sunset. Zephyr Cove also has a campground, a lodge, riding stables, and a handful of little shops, including a general store, nestled along the highway.

Cave Rock

Leaving Zephyr Cove the highway travels almost directly north for some 4 miles, at the end of which one encounters a large promontory — the legendary Cave Rock, Tahoe's most ancient and most noted landmark. The rock has two tunnels passing through it, one naturally formed and the other man-made, with the highway passing through both. The second of these tunnels was built in the early 1900's, and the first was created in times immemorable by the Great Spirit thrusting his lance into the rock. And here is again a romantic version from an Indian legend, relating to the formation of the original cave. According to this legend, there once lived a tribe of Washoe Indians by the rock, fishing and hunting for the most part. The tribe lived in great harmony, and in peace. Then one day, as the story goes, the lake waters began to rise and the tribe scrambled for high ground. But the lake waters continued to rise and the tribespeople scrambled higher, above the rock. And the waters rose higher still. So then the tribespeople looked to the Great Spirit for help, and the Great Spirit responded by thrusting his lance into the rock to form a cave for the waters to drain into. And thus the waters receded and the tribe was saved. But then another problem arose: the water rushing into the cave created a suction into which many of the tribe's fishermen drifted, and were lost. So once again the tribe looked to the Great Spirit for guidance, and the Great Spirit asked the tribesmen to choose the strongest among them for a task of great magnitude. And the tribe chose a brave named "Bo-ha-ra-te". The Great Spirit then placed a large tree-stump by the cave and instructed "Bo-ha-ra-te" to move it across the mouth of the cave every time a fishing boat neared. Thus another disaster was averted, and the tribe lived peacefully once again. (In actual fact, however, Cave Rock is a volcanic neck, formed nearly 5 million years ago.)

Cave Rock is also believed to have been the site of several pitched battles fought between the Washoe and the Paiute, and a legend stemming from this belief tells of a peace-loving people (the Washoe) who were made captive by a cruel, warring tribe (the Paiute), and of how the "god of the world" came to the rescue of the Washoe, creating a cave in the rock in which to imprison the wicked people. The cave then became known as the "Prison of the Genii."

A rest area is now located near the rock, some 200 feet below the highway from where some splendid views of the lake can be enjoyed, as well as excellent inshore fishing along the banks. Of interest, too, is the west face of Cave Rock, on which is outlined the profile of a lady, known as the "Lady of the Lake," with distinctive eye lashes, a delicately upturned nose and a rose-bud mouth. This is best seen from the water when traveling to the rock by boat from the north. A larger profile, that of a gorilla, can be discerned just above the "Lady of the Lake."

There is a small residential community to be found at Cave Rock, and north of there lies Logan Shoals, with a public launching ramp for boating enthusiasts.

North to Glenbrook

From Cave Rock it is 4 miles to historic Glenbrook, the site of Lake Tahoe's first shoreline sawmill, and the largest lumbering settlement in the 1870's and 1880's. In its heyday Glenbrook also boasted one of the lake's most splendid hostelries, the Glenbrook House, while some of the area's finest steamers, including the legendary *Tahoe*, were berthed here too. The settlement was then also visited by such personages as the Presidents Ulysses S. Grant and Rutherford B. Hayes, and humorist Mark Twain. Glenbrook is now a sleepy, privately owned retreat, with a modest 9-hole golf course and some tennis courts.

At Glenbrook, Highway 50 turns east and passes over Spooner Summit, where the Summit Mill, one of the area's earliest lumbermills, was built just prior to 1860. Also, near the Spooner Junction (intersection of Highways 50 and 28) is to be seen the site of the Spooner Station, a Bonanza era hostelry, built in 1863. An enchanting full-day hiking trail now meanders through the state park here. There is a lake to be found here too, known as the Spooner Lake.

Another place of interest, roughly one-half mile southeast of Glenbrook, is the Shakespeare Rock, reached by way of a short walk from the highway. On the face of the rock, almost in the center, there is a faintly discernible, light-colored profile of the famous English playwright, originally discovered by a casual picnicker in the 1860's.

THE EMERALD BAY ROUTE

The Emerald Bay Route comprises essentially the Emerald Bay Road section of Highway 89, from just below the South Tahoe "Y" to the majestic Emerald Bay some 8 miles northwest, plus one or two worthwhile diversions, including Fallen Leaf Lake due south. The route is exceptionally scenic, quite splendid from the moment it leaves the city area. Endless groves of lush evergreens line the highway, punctuated in the fall with bursts of golden poplar; tiny snowmelt creeks are seen toppling in thin, silver strands from the high country, then criss-crossing through the vast wooded meadows below; superb picture-postcard views of the lake are afforded from several points along the highway, especially stunning where the highway hugs the shoreline; and to the west of the road rise a series of noble mountain peaks, including Mount Tallac which is the highest peak on Lake Tahoe's shoreline, and the twin Maggies Peaks. Then, too, there are dozens of beautifully shaded picnic areas and campgrounds encountered along the way, quite randomly, and two places of great historical interest, the Tallac Estates and the fabled Vikingsholm, provide for additional tourist interest. There are even three delightful granite sand beaches to be found along the shoreline here, and a 2½-mile bike path that follows alongside of the highway, crossing over tiny, rustic bridges. Farther west from the route lies the infinitely remote, 63,469-acre Desolation Wilderness, with many enchanting walks to be enjoyed through it, circling scores of miniature fishing lakes. Indeed, this is the most scenic, unspoilt stretch of country at Lake Tahoe, with much to offer the walker as well as the casual motorist-sightseer.

Camp Richardson

Leaving the city area northwest on Emerald Bay Road, one first arrives at Camp Richardson, a lovely picture-book village with one hotel, one store and a handful of other tumbledown structures, all quite unchanged in nearly 50 years. This was once known as "Camp Chipmunk," for the abundance of chipmunks to be found here in the summertime, and later on, in the 1930's and 1940's, it became "the favorite rural residence of city folk" due to its idyllic country setting. Originally in the 1880's, however, Camp Richardson was a logging camp, and also the site of Lake Tahoe's first steam-powered narrow-gauge railroad, the tracks from which can be now viewed at neighboring Tallac Estates. Of interest also are the dozen or so barn-red tourist cabins situated on the lake side of the highway. These were built mostly in the 1930's by one A.L. Richardson, an early day stage-line operator who acquired the acreage in 1923, and for whom the camp is now named. At the fronts of these cabins are to be seen name plaques, each bearing a distinctive name of a bus or motor or other equipment that had served Richardson well during his staging years, such as Nash, Cord, Faegol, Devaux, Fleetwood, Packard, Plymouth, Pierce Arrow, Hall-Scott, and the like. Camp Richardson is also noted for its campground, which boasts 230 well-wooded campsites, and its full-service marina, recently remodeled to accommodate a rambling, on-the-lake restaurant. Well known, too, are the Camp Richardson Stables, from where horseback trail rides can be pursued through the surrounding back woods. A delightful sandy beach, Pope Beach, lies just east of the camp.

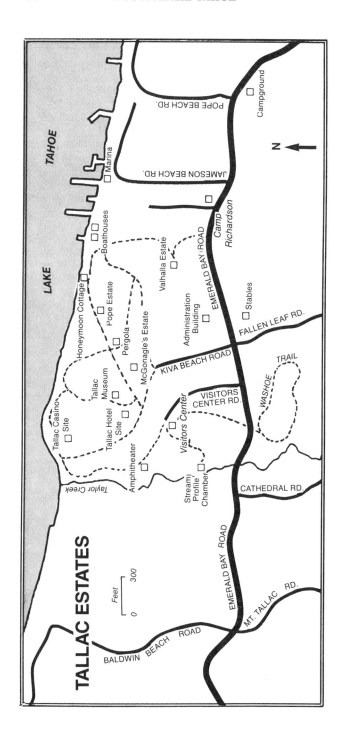

Tallac Estates

Adjoining Camp Richardson on the west are the Tallac Estates — some 2000 acres of meadowland sweeping across from the edge of the camp to Mount Tallac farther west, and south from the Tahoe shoreline to the northern reaches of Fallen Leaf Lake. There are several points of interest here, notable among which is the Kiva Beach Recreation Area, a National Forest preserve situated about three-quarters of a mile west of Camp Richardson, and reached via a small side road, north off the highway. Kiva is a lovely, yellow sand beach, backing onto a magnificent grove of 200-year-old pines, said to be among the oldest such stands of virgin timber in the Tahoe basin. Here amid the pines is also to be seen the site of the legendary Tallac, a palatial three and one-half story hotel, known, in its heyday, as the "Saratoga of the Pacific." It was here that the well-heeled crowds of the 1890's and early 1900's gathered, creating an aura of fantastic high living in the Sierra Nevada. The Tallac was built in 1898 by Elias J. "Lucky" Baldwin, one of the most colorful personalities of his time, whose name is practically synonymous with the Tallac Estates. Much has been said and written about Baldwin over the years, and the tale is often told about how he became "Lucky." According to this, Baldwin, in his younger days, was just a stagecoach captain, with little to his name, save for some worthless mining stock he had earlier acquired in the Comstock for pennies. Then one day, as the story goes, he left on an out-of-area hunting trip, and asked a friend to sell off his stock for whatever it would fetch, for by then it had plummetted to new lows. But as it turned out, the stock certificates were locked up in a safe, the key to which Baldwin had taken with him — an honest error of omission. So the stock remained unsold. And as luck would have it, at about that time the mining company struck a fabulously rich vein of silver, and Baldwin's worthless stock turned into a fortune, almost overnight. Thus returned Elias Jackson Baldwin from his hunting trip a wealthy man, and a lucky one at that; and from that time on he came to be known as "Lucky."

Just to the east of the Tallac site are the historic estates of some notables from South Tahoe's past, including the Popes, the Tevises, the McGonagles, and even the Baldwins. Several graveled walks meander through here, with rock gardens and little streams crossed over by tiny, wooden bridges to be seen here and there, interspersed with a serene pergola or two. Three or four elaborate homes, dating from the early 1900's and featuring wrap-around covered porches and rocked-in fountains, can be toured here as well. A couple of turn-of-the-century boathouses dot the estates' sanded shoreline, with one of them housing the original rail tracks from the historic Camp Richardson Railroad. Situated on the water's edge, too, is a charming "Honeymoon Cottage," built from hand-hewn logs and molded tree limbs, with panoramic glass windows looking out over the lake. Also to be found on the grounds is an ancient but well-preserved log structure that houses the Tallac Museum. This is open to the public during summer, and boasts a wealth of old photographs and other memorabilia from the Tallac past. During summer also, several cultural events, and even a flea market, are featured at the estates.

West of the Kiva Beach Recreation Area lies the U.S. Forest Service Visitors Center, reached via another side road, just 300 feet from the Kiva Beach turnoff. The Visitor Center is especially interesting to nature buffs and children, and has some educational merit. Here one can visit a "stream profile chamber" — a glass-enclosed area at stream level (the stream being Taylor Creek), from where native Kokanee Salmon can be viewed in their natural habitat. Actually, the Kokanee spawn farther upstream, and swim down to the lake in spring, thus May and June are the best months to view them. Also of interest here is a short, 15-minute walk that circles to the back of the Visitor Center and leads to the Taylor Creek inlet point, passing by a miniature amphitheater enroute, where picture slide shows are often featured in the summer; until only a few decades ago, Washoe Indians used to camp by the influx of the creek into the lake. Another worthwhile walk, the "Washoe Trail," which starts out from the Visitor Center parking area and marches across to the south side of the highway, depicts the lifestyles and survival methods of the Washoe Indians, especially interesting to those inclined toward Native American culture.

Southwest from the Visitor Center rises the mighty Mount Tallac, the highest peak on the lake's shoreline, with an elevation of 9785 feet. Tallac means "Great Mountain," and it is for this mountain that the estates are named. The mountain is also noted for its "snow-cross" (a cross-shaped indent filled with snow), which is to be seen on its northeastern face. A rugged trail leads to the base of the mountain, and for the stout of heart there is even a trail scrambling up to the summit. North of Mount Tallac, some three miles away, is to be found another stretch of fine granite sand, the Baldwin Beach.

Fallen Leaf Lake

5 miles south of Emerald Bay Road lies Fallen Leaf Lake, a pleasant little summer retreat, arrived at by taking Fallen Leaf Road — the turnoff for which is to be found almost directly across from the Kiva Beach turnoff — to the very end. Fallen Leaf Lake is actually the second largest alpine lake in the region, second only to Lake Tahoe. It measures three miles by approximately one mile, and has a maximum depth of 420 feet. The lake is believed to have been formed thousands of years ago by a feeder glacier that later joined the main body of ice in the Lake Tahoe trough, and is named for a Delaware chief, "Falling Leaf," who was guide to Colonel John C. "Cockeye" Johnson, the trailblazing pioneer of the Sierra (of Johnson Pass Cutoff fame). An enchanting Indian legend, however, has quite another, rather fascinating version as to the formation and the naming of the lake. According to this legend, an Indian brave fleeing from the Evil One was given a branch of a tree by the Good Spirit, each leaf of which, when dropped on the ground, would create a body of water, thus imposing a barrier before the pursuer. As the Indian fled, crossing over what is now the eastern Sierra range, the Evil One closed in on him. And as the story goes, the Indian panicked, and in his attempt to break off a leaf, he broke off the branch instead, and dropped it on the ground; and in its place sprang the great Lake Tahoe. The Indian continued west. But soon, as he approached Mount Tallac, he looked

back to see that the Evil One had circled the south shore of the lake and was once again closing in on him. So now the Indian dropped that last leaf he still clutched in his hand, and in its place sprang Fallen Leaf Lake. The Indian then safely crossed over into the Valley of the Sacramento, and the lake came to be known as Fallen Leaf, for that magical fallen leaf that had created it.

Fallen Leaf Lake is a more or less self-contained resort, noted for its lodge and campground, both nestled along its southeast corner. The Fallen Leaf Lodge, a brown-shingled two-story building dating from 1913, was built by William Whitman Price, naturalist and Stanford University professor, who ran a boys summer camp in these parts in as early as 1905. A boathouse and marina are located just across from the lodge, and set farther back are several summer cabins, many of them dating from 1911. Both the lodge and cabins are now privately owned, however.

Fallen Leaf is also an excellent fishing lake, and an ideal base from which to explore the idyllic Desolation Wilderness that adjoins to the west. Dozens of secluded trails through the wilderness are accessible from here, including ones to Lily, Heather and the Azure lakes. Southeast of the lake is to be found the Angora Lookout (elevation approximately 7000 feet), which offers breathtaking views of Lake Valley below. A short distance to the west of Fallen Leaf one can visit the Floating Island Lake, where a real floating island is to be seen; the island is said to have provided early day fishermen with a quiet approach when fishing in the tiny lake. Just beyond the floating island, a trail threads past clumps of pine and fir to lead to the base of Mount Tallac in the northwest.

Cascade Lake and Emerald Bay

Returning to the main travel route, Highway 89, we continue west from the Tallac Estates. Here the road begins to climb sharply, weaving in and out of a couple of hairpin bends and skirting the entrances to the Eagle Point and Emerald Bay campgrounds to the south, then passes over a vertical ridge that offers a unique view of two infinitely beautiful bodies of water: Cascade Lake and Emerald Bay.

Cascade Lake, which lies to the south of the ridge and is often to be seen frozen over in winter, is the smaller of the two, measuring one mile by one-half mile. Cascade is picturesque in a rugged sort of way, and in the 1930's and 1940's it attracted Hollywood producers to its shores, providing the setting for some early day wilderness movies, such as *Lightnin'*, starring Will Rodgers, *Rose Marie*, starring Jeannette McDonald and Nelson Eddy, and Dreiser's *A Place in the Sun*. Earlier, in the 1890's and early 1900's, personages such as Mark Twain, John Muir, and Sybil Sanderson, the noted chanteusse, came to stroll the Cascade shores, attracted by its singular beauty; and in 1926, John Steinbeck, then a fledgling student at Stanford, spent the entire summer here. The lake, however, is named for the majestic waterfalls in its southwest corner, seen cascading in 100-foot drops down naked granite ledges to plunge into the lake in a wash of white; these are especially spectacular in the spring, when the feeder stream is full and roiling. The falls actually are known as the White Cloud

Falls, and during the Bonanza Period (1860's) they were the focus of many an artist. Some of the finished canvases featuring these are said to have fetched as much as $2000 — in those days.

In centuries past, Cascade Lake was a favorite campsite of the Washoe Indians. It was then known as "Wa-su-sha-te," meaning "Good Fishing Lake," for its reputation for fishing, at the time, rivalled that of neighboring Fallen Leaf Lake and the smaller Desolation Wilderness lakes. Cascade Lake is also said to have been the scene of a fierce and bloody battle, fought between the Washoe and the Paiute, in which even the women and children are believed to have partaken. Several arrowheads and broken bits of spears have been found here since, mainly in the 1800's. In 1880, even a mummified body of an Indian squaw is reported to have been found buried by the edge of the lake, remarkably well preserved by the extreme cold temperatures of the water. At the time of its discovery, the bloated body, we are told, weighed nearly 300 pounds.

Cascade Lake is now privately owned, the acreage having been first acquired in the mid-1880's by Dr. Charles Brooks Bringham, a famous San Francisco surgeon. It has since passed on to his heirs and family, whose summer homes dot the lake's northeastern shoreline.

Directly above Cascade Lake lies the famous Emerald Bay, acknowledged as "the most beautiful inland harbor in the world." Emerald Bay, quite like the Fallen Leaf and Cascade lakes, was carved out during the ice age by a feeder glacier that eventually joined the main body of ice in Lake Tahoe. The bay is named for its entrancing blue-green waters, and it is today one of the most photographed spots in the Tahoe basin. It is also a favorite destination for the area's cruise boats, which feature year-round Emerald Bay Cruises. In the center of the bay is seen an island, a pinnacled granite outcropping rising some 150 feet from the water. This is Lake Tahoe's only island, variously known as Coquette, Hermit's, Fannette and Emerald Isle. Atop it is perched a one-room stone "tea house," built in about 1930. There is a lovely miniature fireplace to be viewed within. Beside the "tea house" is the site of a long decayed wooden, Gothic tomb, originally built in the 1930's by one Captain Richard Barter, a hard-drinking, hard-swearing English salt, also known as "the Hermit of Emerald Bay." Barter was the caretaker for these Emerald Bay estates for several years, and was notorious for his many boating accidents which inevitably followed his drinking. On one occasion, it is told, he nearly froze to death after his boat capsized just outside the bay. Upon returning to his quarters at the head of the bay, however, he found his toes to be frost-bitten, and is then believed to have amputated them with a kitchen knife. Locals will tell you that on cold, dark nights a wispy mist rises from the bay, almost directly above the island, and that that is the ghost of Captain Barter looking for his tomb.

At the head of Emerald Bay are to be found the Eagle Point Campground and adjoining picnic area, both quite lovely, and to the back of there can be viewed the magnificent Eagle Falls, tumbling in three successive falls down to the lake; the falls are fed by two tiny lakes, Eagle and Granite, located in the high country Desolation Wilderness. The head of the bay also offers some of the most spectacular views of the bay and the lake beyond, especially striking at sunrise when the eastern skies directly across are a flaming amber. It is interesting also

VIKINGSHOLM

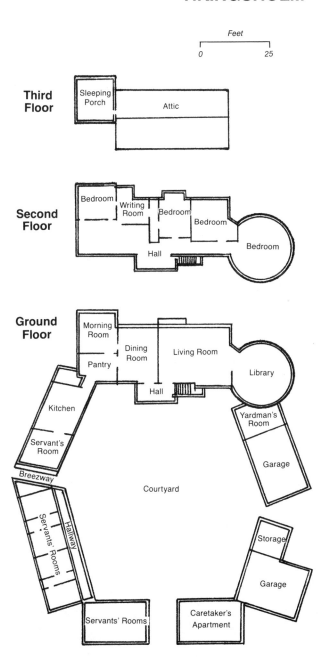

Feet
0   25

Third Floor

Sleeping Porch

Attic

Second Floor

Bedroom

Writing Room

Bedroom

Bedroom

Hall

Bedroom

Ground Floor

Morning Room

Dining Room

Living Room

Pantry

Library

Hall

Kitchen

Servant's Room

Yardman's Room

Garage

Breezway

Courtyard

Servants' Rooms

Hallway

Storage

Garage

Servants' Rooms

Caretaker's Apartment

to note that the road at the head of the bay was the last section of the Rim of the Lake Road to be completed, opening to traffic in 1913. The present highway is actually cut into the face of the lower Maggies Peak, and is often subject to rock avalanches in winter. During its construction, it is told, that several of the out-size boulders had to be blasted four or five times, each, before they would be moved, such was the task of building this section of the road.

Just to the north of the head of the bay is a clearing, used as a car park, from where a mile-long trail descends into the cradle of the bay. It is a somewhat steep trail, but well worth the effort, for at the end of it lies one of Lake Tahoe's greatest treasures: Vikingsholm.

Vikingsholm

Vikingsholm is a masterful replica of a 1200-year-old Viking castle, billed as "the finest example of Scandinavian architecture in North America". Built in 1929 by Lora Josephine Knight, heiress to several fortunes, the castle displays the splendor of an ancient and majestic era. Two turreted towers flank the rock and mortar facade of the main house, and a north and south wing, constructed wholly from wood, extend to the back of the house to form an open courtyard, quite artfully landscaped with rocks and trees. The roofs of the two extension wings are covered with sod, especially picturesque in spring when native wildflowers sprout lavishly upon the sod. In the Viking days the sod served as a form of insulation, and was trimmed by allowing goats to graze upon it. On the east side of the courtyard buildings are seen sharpened rafters jutting out from under the roof, supposedly there to ward off the evil spirits. Also to be seen on some of the extension buildings are "dragon crosses," uniquely Norwegian. These date back a thousand years or more, to when Christianity was first being introduced in the Scandinavian lands; the dragon heads were in fact an accommodation of Norwegian superstitions, and were allowed to remain for that added protection against evil spirits.

During the summer months the State Parks Department conducts tours through the interior of Vikingsholm, with a guide narrating the history of the castle and tales and legends from the Viking era. Within Vikingsholm are to be seen several marvelous duplications of Scandinavian antiques, furniture and other fixtures, and authentic Norwegian weavings. On the ground floor, hanging from the ceiling of the living room are two intricately carved "dragon" beams; in the Viking era the area directly beneath the beams was the exclusive domain of the chieftain and his most honored guests,with women and children being excluded from it. Also in the living room is a lovely, hand-painted "Bridal Chest," given to newlyweds under Norwegian custom, and adorning the living room wall is an exquisite Oriental rug, reportedly purchased for $40,000 in 1929. Farther in, in the hallway stands a life-size wood-carving of a Finnish peasant girl, "Selma," with a clock for its face (a typically Swedish art form). Also in the hallway is a closet door, quite interesting in its fine floral designs. On the upper floor are five individually decorated bedrooms, three of them featuring Norwegian stone fireplaces. Here, too, is a small but interesting "writing room," situated just off the end bedroom, which forms that curious wooden projection seen at the front of the mansion, at the upper right corner; the use of such wooden projections was dominant in early day Norwegian churches.

At the front of Vikingsholm is a boathouse and an L-shaped pier, making the castle accessible by boat as well. Vikingsholm can also be reached by way of a 4-mile trail, the Vikingsholm Trail, which starts out from the adjoining D.L. Bliss State Park to the north, offering some scenic views of the lake enroute.

PRACTICAL INFORMATION FOR
SOUTH LAKE TAHOE

HOW TO GET THERE. By Air. *Air Cal* (800-424-7225) and *Pacific Coast Airlines* (800-322-8811)/235-6967) operate regular flights to South Lake Tahoe from Los Angeles, Burbank, Orange County, Ontario, San Francisco, San Jose, Oakland, Fresno and Seattle. Several other airlines fly to Reno International Airport (see *North Tahoe* section), while at least two companies operate a shuttle-bus service between Reno and South Tahoe.

By Bus. *Greyhound* has daily scheduled services to South Lake Tahoe from most major cities; the *Greyhound Bus Terminal* is situated on Park Avenue, opposite the Crescent V Shopping Center. For reservations and information, call (916) 544-2241.

By Car. The most direct route from San Francisco and Sacramento to the south shore is via Highway 50; the section between Placerville and South Lake Tahoe is especially picturesque during fall. Other approaches to South Tahoe include Highways 395, 88 and 89.

ACCOMMODATIONS. Accommodations in South Lake Tahoe are generally good, friendly and comfortable. There is no shortage of motels and lodges, and several cabins, condominiums and homes, too, are available for vacation rental. Additionally, seasonal packages, such as ski leases, are worth inquiring about. For reservations and information, call (800) 822-5922 in California, or (800) 824-5150 from out of state. Locally, contact the South Lake Tahoe Visitors Bureau at 3066 Lake Tahoe Boulevard, or call them on (916) 544-5050.

Most hotels, motels and lodges in the area accept major credit cards; however, it's best to inquire with each individual establishment. Rates, based on double occupancy, are categorized as follows: *Expensive*, over $40; *Moderate*, $29-$40; *Inexpensive*, under $29. (Note: all rates are subject to change, and are generally 15-25% higher in summer and on weekends and holidays).

Bonanza Route Area

Frontier Lodge. *Moderate.* Located at 3880 Pioneer Trail. 66 rooms, TV, phones, swimming pool, spa. (541-6226)

Olympic Motel. *Moderate*. 3901 Pioneer Trail. 32 units, TV, phones, swimming pool, hot tub. (541-2119)

Pioneer Trail Motel. *Inexpensive*. 3939 Pioneer Trail. 22 units, TV, phones, pool, sauna, spa. (544-5705)

South Shore Inn. *Inexpensive*. 3906 Pioneer Trail. 22 rooms, TV, restaurant. (544-1000)

Three Pines Motel. *Inexpensive*. 3918 Pioneer Trail. 20 rooms, TV. (544-2417).

Stateline Area

Ambassador Motor Lodge. *Moderate*. 4130 Manzanita. 57 rooms, TV, phones, beach, restaurant. (544-6461)

Black Jack Motel. *Moderate*. 985 Park. 24 rooms, TV, phones. (544-3902)

Best Western Station House Inn. *Expensive*. 901 Park. 100 rooms, TV, phones, pool, beach, spa, restaurant. (542-1101)

Blue Jay Motor Lodge. *Moderate*. 4133 Cedar. 65 rooms, TV, pool, beach, phones, restaurant. (544-5231)

Capri Motel. *Moderate*. 932 Stateline. 25 rooms, TV, pool, beach. (544-3665)

Carousel Motel. *Moderate*. 4129 Laurel. 27 rooms, TV, phones. (541-6686)

Carriage House Motel. *Expensive*. 4135 Laurel. 25 rooms, TV. (544-3045)

Casino Area Travel Lodge. *Expensive*. 4003 Highway 50. 66 rooms, TV, phones, pool. (541-5000)

Elm Inn. *Expensive*. 4082 Highway 50. 102 rooms, TV, phones, pool, spa, restaurant. (541-7900)

Fantasy Inn II. *Expensive*. 924 Park. 24 units, TV, phones, pool, in-room spa. (544-6767)

Flamingo Lodge. *Moderate*. 3961 Lake Tahoe Blvd. 90 rooms, TV, phones, pool, spa, sauna, restaurant. (544-5288)

Holiday Lodge. *Moderate*. 4095 Laurel. 148 rooms, TV, phones, pool, sauna. (544-4101)

La Baer Motor Lodge. *Expensive*. 4133 Highway 50. 33 rooms, TV, phones. (544-2139)

Lucky Lodge. *Moderate*. 952 Stateline. 21 rooms, TV, pool, beach. (544-3369)

Mark Twain. *Inexpensive*. 947 Park. 34 rooms, TV, phones, pool, spa, beach. (544-5733)

Pacifica Lodge. *Moderate*. 931 Park, 67 rooms, TV, phones, pool, hot tub. (544-4131)

Playland Motel. *Inexpensive*. 3979 Lake Tahoe Blvd. 30 rooms, TV, pool, spa, beach, restaurant. (544-3862)

Red Carpet Inn. *Expensive*. 4100 Highway 50. 56 rooms, TV, phones, pool, spa, beach, restaurant. (544-2261)

Riviera Inn. *Moderate*. 890 Stateline. 40 rooms, TV, pool. (544-3448)

Royal Valhalla Motel. *Moderate*. 4104 Lake Shore Blvd. 79 rooms, TV, phones, pool, spa, beach. (544-2233)

Shamrock Inn. *Inexpensive*. 4127 Pine. 142 rooms, TV, phones, pool, spa, beach. (541-7150)

Sierra House Inn. *Moderate*. 968 Park. 60 rooms, TV, phones, pool, spa, sauna, beach. (541-4800)

Stardust Lodge. *Expensive*. 4061 Highway 50. 105 rooms, TV, phones, pool, spa, beach. (544-5211)

Stateline Travelodge. *Expensive*. 4011 Highway 50. TV, phones, pool. (544-6000)

Tahoe Colony Inn. *Moderate.* 3794 Montreal. 103 rooms, TV, phones, pool, spa, beach. (544-6481)

Tahoe Driftwood. *Moderate.* 4115 Laurel. 50 rooms, TV, phones, pool, beach, restaurant. (541-7400)

Tahoe Queen Motel. *Inexpensive.* Cnr. Poplar and Manzanita. 29 rooms, TV, phones, pool, spa, beach. (544-2291)

Tahoe West Motor Lodge. *Expensive.* 4082 Pine. 59 rooms, TV, phones, pool, spa, sauna, beach. (544-6455)

Tally Ho Motel. *Moderate.* 4060 Highway 50. 37 rooms, TV, pool, spa, restaurant. (544-3037)

Tradewinds Motel. *Expensive.* 944 Friday Street. 68 rooms, TV, phones, pool, hot tub. (544-6459)

Viking Motor Lodge. *Moderate.* 4083 Cedar. 58 rooms, TV, phones, pool, spa, beach. (541-5155)

City Area

Alta Vista Motel. *Inexpensive.* 3622 Highway 50. 17 rooms, TV. (544-2034)

Blue Lake Motel. *Moderate.* 1055 Ski Run Boulevard. 27 rooms, TV, pool, spa. (544-4853)

Brooke's Lodge. *Moderate.* 3892 Highway 50. 36 rooms, TV, phones, pool. (544-3642)

Condor Lodge. *Expensive.* 3838 Highway 50. 121 rooms, TV, phones, pool, restaurant. (541-5400)

Fantasy Inn I. *Expensive.* 3677 Lake Tahoe Blvd. 32 rooms, TV, phones, in-room spa. (541-6666)

Lakeland Village. *Expensive.* 3535 Lake Tahoe Blvd. 210 units, TV, phones, pool, sauna, hot tub. (541-7711)

Inn by the Lake. *Expensive.* 3300 Highway 50. 100 rooms, TV, phones, pool, sauna and hot tub. (542-0330)

Seven Eleven Motel. *Inexpensive.* 3640 Lake Tahoe Blvd. 21 rooms, TV, phones, spa. (544-3640)

Ski Run Lodge. *Inexpensive.* 1180 Ski Run Blvd. 23 rooms, TV, spa. (544-7622)

South Tahoe Travelodge. *Expensive.* 3489 Highway 50. 59 rooms, TV, phones, pool. (544-5266)

Tahoe Beach and Ski Resort. *Expensive.* 3601 Highway 50. 120 units, TV, phones, pool, spa, hot tub, restaurant. (541-6220)

Tahoe Hacienda. *Moderate.* 3820 Highway 50. 32 rooms, TV, phones, pool, spa. (541-3805)

Tahoe Marina Inn and Condominiums. *Expensive.* Bijou Shopping Center. 76 units, TV, phones, pools, sauna, beach. (541-2180)

Tahoe Seasons Resort. *Expensive.* Keller and Saddle Roads. 160 units, TV, phones, pool, hot tub, restaurant. (541-6700)

Vagabond Tahoe. *Moderate.* 3600 Lake Tahoe Blvd. 200 rooms, TV, phones, pool, spa, sauna, restaurant. (544-3476)

Villa Montreux Motel. *Moderate.* 971 Ski Run Blvd. 36 rooms, TV, phones, pool, beach. (544-3224)

Emerald Bay Road Area

Crystal Range Motel. *Inexpensive.* 941 Emerald Bay Road. 21 rooms, TV. (541-1866)

Emerald Motel. *Inexpensive.* 515 Emerald Bay Road. 9 rooms, TV, pool. (544-5515)

High Country Lodge. *Moderate.* 1227 Highway 50. 15 rooms, TV. (544-0508).

Lazy S Lodge. *Inexpensive.* 609 Emerald Bay Road. 21 rooms, TV, pool, restaurant. (541-0230)

Matterhorn Motel. *Moderate.* 2187 Highway 50. 18 rooms, TV, phones, pool. (541-0367)

Pine Cone Acres. *Moderate.* 735 Emerald Bay Road. 20 rooms, TV, pool. (541-0375)

Silver Shadows Lodge. *Moderate.* 1251 Highway 50. 18 rooms, TV, pool, hot tub. (541-3575)

Star Lake Motel. *Inexpensive.* 2446 Highway 50. 17 rooms, TV, pool. (544-6776)

Tahoe Sundowner Motel. *Inexpensive.* 121 Highway 50. 16 rooms, TV, restaurant. (541-2282)

Tahoe Valley Motel. *Moderate.* Highway 50 and Tahoe Keys Blvd. 21 rooms, TV, phones, spa, sauna, restaurant. (541-0353)

Washoe Motel. *Inexpensive.* 751 Emerald Bay Road. 16 rooms, TV, pool, restaurant. (541-1141)

TELEPHONE AND EMERGENCY. The South Lake Tahoe telephone area code is 916 for the California side, and 702 for the Nevada side. In an emergency, dial "O" - Operator.

Specific emergency services include — *South Lake Tahoe Fire Department* (916) 541-1226; *Douglas County Fire Department* (702) 588-5121; *Kingsbury Fire Department* (702) 588-3111; *South Lake Tahoe Police* (916) 541-4060; *South Lake Tahoe Sheriff* (916) 544-3464; *Douglas County Sheriff* (702) 588-3511; *Ambulance* (916) 541-3333; *Poison Center* (800) 852-7221.

Also of importance: *Barton Memorial Hospital* (916) 541-3420; *California Highway Patrol* (916) 577-1001; *Coast Guard* (916) 583-4433; *Road Conditions,* California (916) 577-3550; *Road Conditions,* Nevada (702) 793-1313.

TOURIST INFORMATION. *South Lake Tahoe Visitors Bureau,* 3066 Lake Tahoe Boulevard (Highway 50), South Lake Tahoe; (916) 544-5050. *South Lake Tahoe Chamber of Commerce,* 3066 Lake Tahoe Boulevard; (916) 541-5255. *Tahoe-Douglas Chamber of Commerce,* 175 Highway 50, Stateline; (702) 588-4591.

The useful weekly publication, *Lake Tahoe Action* (freely available outside most area stores), provides information on current tourist activities and shows at the hotel-casinos in town. Also worthwhile is the bimonthly *Key* magazine, available at the Chambers of Commerce, which contains show information and shopping tips mostly.

HOW TO GET AROUND. By Bus. The city is serviced by *STAGE* (South Tahoe Area Ground Express). A regular 24-hour schedule is maintained between the Stateline and the South Tahoe Y, and scheduled stops are made at marked bus-stops on Lake Tahoe Boulevard (Highway 50); however, buses may be flagged on any street serviced by the *STAGE* bus system, except the boulevard. For timetable and information, call (916) 544-2266.

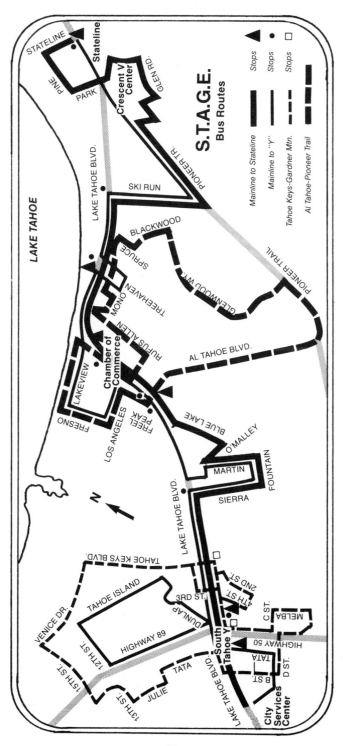

LAKE TAHOE

STATELINE

PINE
PARK
Stateline

Crescent V Center

GLEN RD.

SKI RUN

LAKE TAHOE BLVD.

BLACKWOOD

SPRUCE

MONO
TREEHAVEN

RUFUS ALLEN

CHAMBER of Commerce

LAKEVIEW

FRESNO

LOS ANGELES

FREEL PEAK

PIONEER TR.

AL TAHOE BLVD.

GLENWOOD WY.

PIONEER TRAIL

BLUE LAKE

O'MALLEY

MARTIN

FOUNTAIN

SIERRA

LAKE TAHOE BLVD.

N

VENICE DR.

TAHOE KEYS BLVD.

TAHOE ISLAND

3RD ST.
DUNLAP

HIGHWAY 89

12TH ST.

15TH ST.

13TH ST.

JULIE

TATA

South Tahoe Y

4TH ST.
2ND ST.

C ST.

MELBA

HIGHWAY 50

TATA
B ST.
D ST.

City Services Center

S.T.A.G.E.
Bus Routes

	Stops
▲	
•	Stops
□	Stops

— Mainline to Stateline

— Mainline to "Y"

- - - Tahoe Keys-Gardner Mtn.

▪ ▪ ▪ Al Tahoe-Pioneer Trail

47

By Taxi. The metropolitan area enjoys the services of both the *South Tahoe Yellow Cabs* (916) 541-4141 and *Dial-a-Ride* (916) 577-5000; the latter also offers charters, tours and a host of other services, employing cars, buses and limousines.

By Car. Car rentals are available at *Alpine Rent-A-Car* (916) 577-2727; *National Car Rental System* (702) 588-3629/Harvey's Hotel and (916) 541-2277/Lake Tahoe Airport; *Tahoe Rent-A-Car* (916) 544-4500; *Bob's Arrow Rent-R-Car* (916) 544-0627; *Budget* (916) 541-5777/(702) 588-5145; *Aspen Car Rentals* (916) 541-4613; *Hertz* (702) 588-4911; *Dollar Rent A Car* (702) 588-4849; and *Lloyd's International Rent A Car* (916) 544-1662. Most car rental agencies also rent four-wheel drives, with snow tires, chains and ski-racks.

If you are driving in the area in winter time, a word of advice: "winterize" your car; always carry tire-chains, and use them when the conditions so require; DO NOT park on any public street, or in any other "snow-plow" area — it's against the law; watch out for ice, especially black ice; and generally, exercise due caution, and take extra care when driving in winter conditions.

Other Modes of Transport. Shuttle-bus services are available to most ski areas, and courtesy buses to and from casinos; inquire at your motel, or call the respective casino or ski area. *Lake Tahoe Cruises* (916) 541-4652 offers across-the-lake transport to the north shore much of the year; and *See Tahoe Tours* (702) 832-0713, as well as *LTR* (702) 323-4511, operate shuttle bus services between South Lake Tahoe and the Reno International Airport.

SEASONAL EVENTS. The South Lake Tahoe winter season is dominated by skiing and ski events, such as: *the South Lake Tahoe Winter Carnival* at the Sierra Ski Ranch (**January**); the *Media Cup Ski Race* at the Kirkwood Ski Resort, and the *John Denver Celebrity Ski Classic* at Heavenly Valley (**February**); *St. Patrick's Day Celebrations* at the Echo Summit Ski area, and the *Echo Summit to Kirkwood Cross-Country Ski Race* (**March**); the *USSA Silver Dollar Downhill* at Heavenly Valley, and the *Annual Para-Ski Meet* at Kirkwood (**April**).

In **May**, as the snow melts and the rivers swell, the *White Water Week* gets underway — and the focus of attention is Markleeville, California (southwest of Meyers), which provides some incredible, heart-stopping white water rafting down the Carson River.

June. The *Wagon Train Festival*; a wagon train comprising 30 authentic 19th century wagons rolls through town enroute to Placerville and Sacramento, a replay of yesteryear. The event is characterized by street dancing and other festivities. Also, the *Southern Crossing Sailboat Race* and the home-grown *Tahoe Wild West Week* are at about this time.

July. The *Star Spangled Fourth* celebrations light up the city, while the Kirkwood Ski Resort, which usually still has snow at this time, plays host to the *Avalanche Cup Ski Race*. Also, the annual *Lake Tahoe Sail Week* gets underway, and the *Sierra Nevada Open Golf Tournament* is held at the Edgewood Golf Course, right next to the Stateline.

August. The Amacker Ranch at Tahoe Paradise (Meyers) hosts the annual rodeo.

September. The *World's Toughest Triathlon* winds through a gruelling 148.6-mile course, covering both the South Tahoe area and part of the east shore. And in the middle of the month, neighboring Virginia City hosts the annual *Camel Races*.

October. The South Lake Tahoe Chamber of Commerce holds its annual golf tournament.

December. If you are in the area on New Year's Eve, don't miss the *Torchlight Parade* at Kirkwood Ski Resort, nor the elaborate celebrations at the Stateline, South Lake Tahoe.

For exact dates, and detailed information on events, contact the *South Lake Tahoe Visitors Bureau* at (916) 544-5050. The Bureau also publishes a "Calendar of Events" — available free upon request.

TOURS. *Grayline* has coach tours of Lake Tahoe and historic Virginia City, May through September. The *Rim of the Lake Tour,* which will show you around the entire lake, including giving you a preview of the fabled Ponderosa Ranch, lasts 4 hours and costs $20.00 per person; the *Virginia City Tour* costs $19.00, and takes 5 hours. Call (702) 588-6688 for information and reservations.

For information on other bus and jeep tours, contact the *Visitors Bureau* on (916) 544-5050; and for scenic flights from the Lake Tahoe Airport, call *Executive Aero Systems* on (916) 541-7820.

PLACES OF INTEREST. Pioneer Trail. The trail runs just to the southwest of the city area, from Meyers to more or less the Stateline; look for the turnoff past Meyers, on the east side of the road. This is the original Placerville-Carson Back Road, upon which passed the mammoth deluge of miners and prospectors in the Bonanza Days of the 1860's. Sites of the Bonanza era waystations and hostelries are indicated by numbered wooden markers. A worthwhile guide to these sites if the Lake Tahoe Historical Society publication, "Lake Valley's Past." See also the *Pioneer Trail* section earlier in this book for map and details.

Historical Society Museum. Near the South Lake Tahoe Chamber of Commerce in Al Tahoe, on Hwy 50. Artifacts from Lake Valley's early days, some of Indian origin; and several old photographs depicting Lake Tahoe's history. Worth viewing too is a 1920's bobsled and two or three pieces of 19th century farm machinery. Open summers 10-4.

Osgood's Toll House. Corner of Hwy 50 and Rufus Allen Blvd. in Al Tahoe. A dark-brown weathered cabin, 40 feet square, originally built in 1859 and located at the foot of the Meyers Grade; this is South Tahoe's oldest building today. It was moved to its present location in the early 1970's and propped on pilings. Can only be viewed from outside.

Globin's Resort. In Al Tahoe, on Lakeview and Sacramento Streets. Built mostly in 1924, the resort comprises the Globin Home, a red-brick building situated just above the Regan Beach at the intersection of the two streets, and a handful of cottages scattered farther back on Sacramento St.; the home sits on the site of the original Al Tahoe Hotel. These are now private residences.

Lake Tahoe Airport. About a mile south of the South Tahoe Y, off Hwy 50. A splendid mountain airport, dating from 1959.

Ski Run Marina. At the lake end of Ski Run Blvd., just south of Hwy 50. Noted mostly for the *Tahoe Queen,* a Mississippi paddlewheeler, that berths here. Lake cruises can be taken from here year-round.

Heavenly Valley Aerial Tram. Located at Heavenly's California Base Lodge (follow signs from Ski Run Blvd., south off Hwy 50, to the ski resort). A 50-passenger tram car takes you to the *Top of the Tram* restaurant, some 2000 feet above lake level, offering some of the most gorgeous views of the lake and surrounding mountains. The cars travel along 1400 feet of cable to achieve a vertical rise of 1700 feet; time taken is 3 minutes 38 seconds one way. The tram operates year-round. Also visit the ski area, "America's largest alpine ski resort," sprawled over 20 square miles, nine mountains and two states.

Casino District. At the Stateline, on the Nevada side. A half-mile glitter strip, this is home to some of Tahoe's finest hotel-casinos, including *Harrah's, Harvey's, Caesar's* and the *High Sierra*. Here is to be found non-stop gambling action and some of the best in big name entertainment. The district is an absolute must for visitors to the area.

Friday's Station. Corner of Hwy 50 and Loop Road, set slightly back from the highway. A charming, beautifully restored Bonanza era hostelry and Pony Express remount station, originally built in 1860. A private residence now.

Kingsbury Grade. Southeast of the Stateline casinos, off Hwy 50; the grade actually forms part of Nevada Route 207. Drive up the grade to Daggett Summit (elev. 7375 feet), then down the Haines Canyon in a more or less vertical drop, and into the Carson Valley; the descent is approx. 3000 feet, achieved in just over 6 miles. This is one of the most spectacular drives at the lake, with great views of both Carson Valley and Lake Tahoe.

Zephyr Cove. 4 miles north of Stateline. This is mostly a summer resort, with a marina and a sandy beach. Home port of *M.S. Dixie*, a glass-bottomed Mississippi river boat. Cruise on board the *Dixie* year-round; visit also Zephyr Cove Stables for scenic trail rides. Open May-Oct.

Cave Rock. An ancient Tahoe landmark, 2 miles north of Zephyr Cove, on Hwy 50. Two tunnels pass through the rock and the highway passes through the tunnels. Nearby is a pleasant little rest area.

Historic Tallac Estates. Situated between Camp Richardson and *Kiva Beach Recreation Area*, off Hwy 89; reached via Kiva Beach Rd. Park at Kiva and explore on foot. Tour some splendid 1920's homes, including the *Pope-Tevis Estate*, the *McGonagles Estate*, and the *Baldwin Estate*. Visit also the *Tallac Museum* and *Tallac* site. Open June-Sept.

Visitors Center. Also off Hwy 89; look for turnoff 300 feet past Kiva Beach turnoff. Visit *Stream Profile Chamber,* an enclosed viewing area at stream (Taylor Creek) level, which shows off native fish in their natural habitat; in spring and fall, watch giant Kokanee Salmon as they swim downstream. Two or three worthwhile walks, mostly 15-30 minute ones, can be taken through here too; notable are the *Washoe* and *Rainbow* trails. Open June-Sept.

Emerald Bay State Park. Approximately 8 miles north of South Lake Tahoe, on Hwy 89. Here is seen the beautiful blue-green oval of Emerald Bay, billed as "the most beautiful inland harbor in the world." Several splendid views of the lake are obtained from just above the bay. Some enjoyable walks and a handful of campgrounds and picnic areas, including the Eagle Falls rest area, just back from the bay; the falls are especially picturesque in spring. Also visit the fabled *Vikingsholm* in the cradle of the bay, reached via a mile-long hike from the parking area on the northwest corner. *Vikingsholm* is a masterful replica of a 1200-year-old Viking castle, acknowledged as "the finest example of Scandinavian architecture in North America." Tours of the 38-room castle are conducted by State Park personnel in summer. Some lovely Scandinavian antiques and furniture are seen within, as well as Norwegian weavings, a Swedish wood-carving, and several ornate fixtures. A booklet entitled "Vikingsholm" is to be recommended for further reading. Open July-Aug. 10-4.

Fallen Leaf Lake. A self-contained summer resort, 5 miles west of South Tahoe; reached via Fallen Leaf Road, the turnoff for which lies just past Camp Richardson, off Hwy 89. View Fallen Leaf Lodge, built in 1913. Opportunities for camping, hiking, fishing, boating and horseback riding. Open May-Sept.

Art Galleries. *Sierra Galleries*, at Caesar's Tahoe Hotel-Casino, Stateline; bronze sculptures and paintings. *Curtis Art Gallery*, located in the Round Hill Mall, Round Hill. *Thomas Art Gallery*, located on Echo Summit just off Hwy. 50; boasts an array of authentic Indian artifacts and paintings.

NEARBY ATTRACTIONS. Carson City, Nevada. This is the nation's smallest state capital, population 15,000. It is located 27 miles northeast of South Lake Tahoe, reached via Hwy. 50 east; or Hwy. 395. The town enjoys a lovely setting, more or less at the foot of the eastern Sierra, and has several historic buildings and Victorian mansions, many of them beautifully restored. Of particular interest is the *Governor's Mansion*, situated on Mountain Street. Visit also the *Nevada State Museum*, considered to be one of the finest museums in the West; it is housed in the old U.S. Mint building, dating from 1866, where silver was coined during the Comstock era. A wealth of 19th century artifacts and the controversial "Fremont Cannon" are on display at the museum. Other places of interest here are the *State Capitol*, the *State Library* and the *Legislative Building*, all of which are open to the public during the week. Also interesting from the tourist standpoint are the *Old Virginia & Truckee Railroad Shop*, located at the corner of Stewart and Washington Streets, and the *Nevada State Supreme Court* on Carson Street. Just south of Carson City lies the *Railroad Museum*, where antique trains and steam engines are being restored. Worth visiting too is the *Ormsby House Hotel-Casino*, a long-standing institution, once owned by U.S. Senator Paul Laxalt. The *Carson City Visitors Center* is to be found in the Carson Shopping Mall, just south of town; self-guided maps with histories and detailed information on several restored homes are available at the center.

Gardnerville and Minden. These twin townships are nestled in the Carson Valley some 18 miles from South Lake Tahoe, reached by way of Kingsbury Grade (Rt. 207) and Hwy. 395. Gardnerville is noted for its Basque influence, with some excellent Basque food restaurants to be found there. At Minden visit *Sharkey's Casino*, where several antique slot machines and rodeo king, Casey Tibbs' saddles and old photographs can be viewed, as well as some authentic Indian Chief portraits.

Genoa. This is the oldest town in Nevada, first settled in 1849 by a group of Mormons. The town is situated roughly 12 miles from South Lake Tahoe, arrived at by taking the Kingsbury Grade (Route 207) to the bottom, then Foothill Road north. Of interest at Genoa is gaming pioneer *Harvey Gross' Ranch*, where a herd of real live bison can be seen. Also, just south of Genoa is to be found *Walley's Hot Springs Resort*, dating from 1862; there are some worthwhile hot mineral spas at the resort.

See also *Nearby Attractions* in the *North Lake Tahoe* section.

LAKE CRUISES. One of the most enjoyable ways of seeing the lake is on board a cruise boat. South Lake Tahoe has two of the largest cruise boats at the lake, and one or two smaller craft, all offering scheduled Emerald Bay Cruises, Sunset Dinner and Dance Cruises, and a host of other cruises of varying lengths and descriptions.

M.S. Dixie. This is the lake's oldest cruise boat, berthed at the Zephyr Cove Marina, 4 miles north of the Stateline. It made its debut on the lake in 1947, and has since ferried hundreds of thousands of passengers around the lake. The "Dixie" is a 350-passenger, glass-bottomed Mississippi riverboat, with a giant red paddlewheel at its stern; the glass-bottom viewing area offers some extraordinary opportunities. Daily *Emerald Bay Cruises* can be taken on board the " M.S. Dixie"; cost: $10.00 adults, $4.00 children. The *Sunset Dinner and Dance Cruises* are $24.00-$26.00 (dinner inclusive). Other cruises include the *South Shore Cruise* and the *Champagne Brunch Cruise*. Also available are charters for private parties, weddings and other special occasions. For information and reservations, call (702) 588-3508/(702) 882-0786.

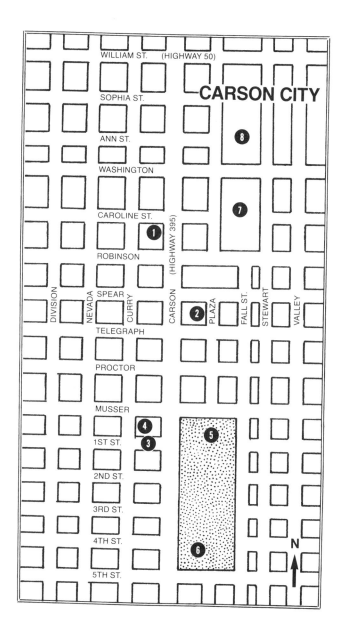

CARSON CITY

WILLIAM ST. (HIGHWAY 50)
SOPHIA ST.
ANN ST.
WASHINGTON
CAROLINE ST.
ROBINSON
SPEAR
TELEGRAPH
PROCTOR
MUSSER
1ST ST.
2ND ST.
3RD ST.
4TH ST.
5TH ST.

DIVISION
NEVADA
CURRY
CARSON (HIGHWAY 395)
PLAZA
FALL ST.
STEWART
VALLEY

N

Points of Interest –
1) Nevada State Museum
2) Nevada State Library
3) Nevada State Supreme Court
4) Fire Department & Museum
5) State Capitol
6) State Legislative Building
7) Post Office and Federal Building
8) Old V & T Shop

Tahoe Queen. Berthed at the Ski Run Marina in the city, the "Tahoe Queen" is owned and operated by *Lake Tahoe Cruises*. This is actually one of the most colorful and best known of Lake Tahoe's cruise boats. This is also a large Missisippi river-boat type vessel, with white-lace trim and an out-size paddlewheel at its stern; it has a glass-bottom viewing area too. The "Queen" sails daily to beautiful Emerald Bay, with live commentary and live music being offered on most of its cruises. Cost of *Emerald Bay Day Cruise*: $11.00/adults, $4.50/children; cost of *Sunset Dinner and Dance Cruise*: $31.00/adults (dinner included). *Lake Tahoe Cruises* also offers charters for groups, parties, weddings and other occasions, as well as a *Squaw Valley Shuttle* ($16.50 round trip). Reservations suggested (916) 541-3364.

Miss Tahoe. A smaller vessel with a more contemporary design, this is also operated by *Lake Tahoe Cruises*, though berthed at the Lakeside Marina near the Stateline, at the bottom end of Park Avenue. Cost of *Emerald Bay Day Cruise*: $11.00/adults, $4.50 children; cost of *Sunset Dinner and Dance Cruise* $31.00. Also available are private charters. Reservations and information (916) 541-3364.

Spirit of Tahoe Keys. Operated by the *Tahoe Executive Charter Corporation* out of the Tahoe Keys Marina, this often offers *Gambler's Specials* to the Hyatt Hotel-Casino on the north shore. For the most part, however, the *Charter Corporation* specializes in personalized charters. Phone: (916) 541-5053.

Woodwind. This is of course the lake's largest sailing vessel, a trimaran, also berthed at Zephyr Cove Marina, north of the Stateline. Some memorable cruises can be enjoyed on board the "Woodwind," sailing quite randomly into the sunsets. Daily excursions are offered between May 1 and October 31, and weekend trips through the rest of the year; cost: $9.00/adults, $4.50/children; and for *Sunset Champagne Cruises*: $16.00/adults. Private charters for weddings and parties are also available. Reservations (702) 588-3000.

RAFTING. There is some rafting on the Upper Truckee River, starting out from near the Highway 50 bridge in the Tahoe Paradise (Meyers) area. But most keen rafters, particularly whitewater enthusiasts, prefer the neighboring Carson and American Rivers. The Carson, especially, offers some of the most thrilling white water at the peak of the snow-melt; the 8-mile section between Silver Creek and Markleeville is perhaps one of its wildest stretches.

Much of the Carson River rafting is centered in Markleeville, some 28 miles south of Lake Tahoe. The 20-mile stretch of river between Markleeville and Gardnerville offers some of the most picturesque rafting in the region — with untouched wilderness, riverside hot-springs, a promise of fish, and great mountain views. Day as well as overnight trips are available along this stretch.

West of the river Carson, the American River provides a variety of both rapids and calms. Again, rafting on this river is at its best in spring and early summer.

For more information on rafting trips and equipment rentals and sales, contact any of these commercial rafting guides: *Head Water Rafting*, Stateline (702) 588-3002; *Chili Bar White Water Tours*, Placerville (916) 622-6104; *Little Switzerland's Wet Fantasies*, Tahoe Paradise (916) 577-5646; *Wild River Rafting Company*, Tahoe Paradise (916) 577-7238. For rafts and accessories, contact *The Outdoorsman*, South Lake Tahoe; (916) 541-1660.

FISHING. Although enormously popular in summer, fishing has been steadily gaining ground as a year-round sport at South Lake Tahoe. A variety of trout (including Mackinaw, Rainbow, Cutthroat, Brook, Brown and Golden), Kokanee Salmon, and whitefish flourish in the south shore waters; even the feeder tributaries are blessed with an abundant supply. All you need in order to go out and get them, is the appropriate gear, a valid California or Nevada fishing license, and a word of caution: specifically, you may not fish within 200 yards of the mouth of any tributary to or from the lake, spearfishing and use of live bait other than game fish taken from the lake is prohibited, and catch is limited to five game fish, five trout, five salmon, and five Mountain Whitefish. Complete information on legalities and illegalities of fishing in Lake Tahoe can be found in the "Angler's Guide" booklet, which is available from the *Department of Fish and Game* — Box 10678, Reno, Nevada, (702) 784-6214; or Box 73, Tahoe City, California, (916) 583-3325.

FISHING GUIDES. Year-round fishing charters and guide services are available at *George's Fishing Trips,* Stateline (588-5927); *Lake Tahoe Excursions & Sport Fishing,* South Lake Tahoe (541-7177); *Bruce Hernandez,* South Tahoe (577-2246); *Dennis' Fishing Charters,* South Tahoe (577-6834); *Tahoe Sports Fishing,* South Tahoe (541-5448).

FISHING HOT SPOTS. Following are some of the favorite fishing spots, where, more often than not, fish are known to "bite." However, for the most current information on where they're biting, and the best lure and bait, ask at your local fish and tackle shop or marina.

Rubicon Point. Off the northern tip of the D.L. Bliss State Park, extending nearly a mile south; Kokanee salmon are plentiful at depths of 80 feet (June-September).

Emerald Point. At tne mouth of Emerald Bay, close into the shore, toplining is favored for Rainbows and Browns.

Southwest Corner. A mile out from the Baldwin and Kiva beaches, Kokanee are plentiful; and just east of there, inshore fishing is promising.

Buoy Run. Out from the Al Tahoe shoreline, deepline fishing at depths of 60-200 feet is suggested.

Ski Run. Just north from the Bijou shore, deepline at depths of 100-400 feet.

Hobart Hole. Opposite Nevada Beach, just south of Elk Point; excellent Mackinaw at depths of around 60 feet.

Zephyr Cove Run. In the Zephyr Cove area; deepline at depths of 100-400 feet.

East Shore. From Cave Rock north to nearly Glenbrook Bay; inshore fishing is excellent, some of the best at the lake.

Desolation Wilderness Lakes. Most of the area's 80 lakes are blessed with Brooks, Browns, Goldens and Rainbows.

Fallen Leaf Lake. Browns, Mackinaw, Rainbows, and Kokanee are abundant.

Lower Echo Lake. Rainbow trout and Kokanee salmon remain native to this lake.

HIKING. South Tahoe offers some of the most exciting hiking opportunities for miles around. The Desolation Wilderness, situated off the southwest shore of the lake, alone has more than ten different hiking trails snaking through its 63,469-acre spread; while at least 20 vastly varied trails, mainly day hikes, wind through other parts of the

National Forest and State Park lands. A "wilderness permit" is required prior to entering the wilderness area; there is no cost for such permits, though overnight permits are subject to a quota system, and advance reservations are advised. For permits and any additional information, contact the *Lake Tahoe Basin Management Unit*, South Lake Tahoe (541-1130); or, *El Dorado National Forest*, Placerville (622-5061); or, the *Pacific Ranger Station*, Pollock Pines (644-2348).

HIKING TRAILS. Although a complete list of the region's hiking trails, together with maps, can be obtained from the *Forest Service* or the *South Lake Tahoe Chamber of Commerce*, the following list provides a sampling of the more popular trails:

Emerald Bay Area. *Eagle Falls Trail.* From the Eagle Falls Picnic Area, a steep ascent leads into the Desolation Wilderness, with Eagle Lake being reached at the end of it; beautiful views of the basin are afforded enroute. It's a 2-mile round trip, taking approximately 1½ hours.

Bayview Trail. Also a steep trail, it begins at the back of Bayview Picnic Area; the trail offers some spectacular views of Lake Tahoe. Allow 2 hours for this 2 mile round trip.

Vikingsholm Trail. From the "view parking" just north of Eagle Falls, the trail descends into the cradle of Emerald Bay, leading to the famed Vikingsholm Castle built by Mrs. Lora Knight in 1929; the castle is open to public between 10 a.m. and 4 p.m., summers. 1 mile, 1 hour each way.

Rubicon Trail. The trail starts out at the Vikingsholm Castle in Emerald Bay and traces the periphery of the lake to a point at the north end of the D.L. Bliss State Park. It's a 4½-mile trail that's likely to use up the better part of a day.

Balancing Rock and Lighthouse Trails. Both are short, self-guided trails through the northern part of the D.L. Bliss State Park — one, a ½ mile trail, leads to the Balancing Rock, while the other, a ¼ mile hike, will take you to the site of an old lighthouse above Rubicon Point.

Visitors Center Area. *Washoe Trail.* This trail begins at the end of the Visitors Center parking lot, and it is interesting in so much as it depicts the Washoe Indians' lifestyle and methods of survival. Estimated duration: 30 minutes.

Taylor Creek Trail. Begin on the Washoe Trail, then branch off onto a path alongside the creek; the trail follows alongside of the creek to the north shore of Fallen Leaf Lake. ¼ mile; 30 minutes.

Lake of the Sky Trail. From the back of the Visitor Center, the trail winds past a small amphitheather and down to the Lake Tahoe shoreline. ¼ mile long; 15 minutes.

Fallen Leaf Lake Area. *Floating Island Trail.* A sign-posted trailhead is situated ½ mile in from Highway 89, on Spring Creek Road. The trail follows the eastern slopes of Mount Tallac to Floating Island Lake, where there's a real floating island site to be seen. This is a 2 mile long trail, expected to take 1½ hours.

Angora Lakes Trail. From the end of Angora Lakes Road, south of Fallen Leaf Lake, a short, uphill, wooded trail leads to the twin Angora Lakes; swimming and fishing are available at the lakes. ½ mile trail; 20 minutes.

Frederick's Trail. Starting out at Fallen Leaf Road, ¼ mile south of the Fallen Leaf Campground, the trail leisurely traces a loop, offering a meadowland solitude. 1¼ mile loop, estimated to take 1½ hours.

Grass Lake Trail. From Fallen Leaf Lake drive down Glen Alpine Road to Lily Lake; the trail begins at Lily Lake and winds past the famous Glen Alpine Springs to Grass Lake, which is situated inside the Desolation Wilderness area. 2 miles of trail; 1½ hours.

Gilmore Lake Trail. Follow the Grass Lake trail to Glen Alpine Springs, then branch off along the northwest trail; a modest climb leads to Gilmore Lake at the base of Mount Tallac. Allow a full day for this 4-mile hike.

Susie Lake/Heather Lake Trail. Also via Glen Alpine Springs, this trail snakes through 4 miles of rugged country to Susie Lake, which is situated in the wilderness, and continues another mile to Heather Lake. Expect to utilize a full day.

Mount Tallac Trail. There are two different approaches to the summit: one through Glen Alpine, and the other via the Floating Island. The Glen Alpine Route is 6 miles long, with a gradual climb, while the Floating Island route is only 4 miles, but substantially steeper. Either way, allow a full day for a hike to the top.

Echo Lakes Area. *Echo Lakes Trail.* Skirting both Upper and Lower Echo lakes is a 2-mile trail that takes approximately 1½ hours to complete. A boat hire is also available between the two lakes. Parking is available at Lower Echo Lake, at the end of Echo Lakes Road.

Tamarack Lake Trail. Follow the Echo Lakes trail, a mile past Upper Echo, to Tamarack Lake. It's a 3-mile trail that can be reduced to a third of its length by use of a boat across the two Echo Lakes.

Lake Aloha Trail. Again, follow the Echo Lakes trail, first to Tamarack Lake, then 3 miles further to the man-made Lake Aloha — one of the largest lakes in the Desolation Wilderness Area. 6 miles each way; requires a full day.

Hawley Grade Trail. From Echo Summit this trail descends to the Upper Truckee River, offering magnificent views of South Lake Tahoe. Originally a wagon road, built by one Asa H. Hawley in 1854, this trail once represented the first "reasonable descent" into Lake Valley. The trail is 2½ miles long, and takes just over 2 hours.

Meiss Lake Country. Situated some 6 miles south of Tahoe Paradise (Meyers), this trail system comprises several miles of trails and lakes. A sign-posted trailhead is located nearly 5 miles south of Highway 50, leading to trails of varied lengths and durations.

 BICYCLING. Many miles of bike trails can be found on the south shore. Bike rentals are easily available from the outdoor lots on Emerald Bay Road, just north of the Y.

Other bike rental outlets in the area include — *Tahoe Bike Shop,* South Lake Tahoe (916) 544-8060; *The Clean Machine,* South Lake Tahoe (916) 544-2453; *Sierra Cycle Works,* South Lake Tahoe (916) 541-7505.

For bicycle sales and repairs, visit *The Outdoorsman Bike Shop* on Hwy. 50, South Lake Tahoe (916) 541-1660.

 **BEACHES AND PICNIC AREAS.** The south shore has some of the finest beaches at the lake — nine of them, mostly granite sand; fire pits and restroom facilities are available at several of these, and a nominal parking fee of around a dollar is not uncommon. Picnic areas abound.

BEACHES. *Baldwin Beach.* Off Highway 89, 1½ miles northwest of Camp Richardson. Facilities include picnic area, swimming area, fire pits, restrooms and parking; no dogs or boats are permitted on the beach.

Kiva Beach. Just north of Visitors Center, with the forest bordering on it; sign-posted turn-off. Picnic areas, fire pits, restrooms and parking are available.

Pope Beach. A mile east of Kiva Beach; access via Pope Beach Road, just east of Camp Richardson. Picnic area, fire pits, and restrooms and parking facilities are available; no dogs or boats.

Barton Beach. Between Tahoe Keys and Lakeview Avenue (east of Tahoe Keys). This is one of the smaller beaches, accessible only by boat. Facilities are limited to restrooms, swimming area and a lifeguard; boats are permitted, except in the marked swimming area.

Regan Beach. Located at the foot of Sacramento Avenue, just over Lakeview Avenue, in Al Tahoe. Picnic area, swimming area, grass area, restrooms, parking, concession stand, play equipment, wind-surfing rentals, and on-duty lifeguard (summers, between 11 a.m. and 6 p.m.). No dogs, fires, or alcohol permitted on beach.

El Dorado Beach. Almost adjacent to Reagan Beach, abutting Lake Tahoe Boulevard (Highway 50) across from the City Campground and the South Lake Tahoe Chamber of Commerce. Picnic area, swimming area, lifeguard, boat ramp, parking, and restrooms.

Connolly Beach. Behind the Timber Cove Lodge, at the end of Bal Bijou Road. Swimming area, lifeguard, concession stand, restrooms, and limited parking.

Nevada Beach. Off Highway 50, south of Elk Point (near Round Hill). Picnic area, swimming area, fire pits, and restroom and parking facilities.

Zephyr Cove. North of Round Hill, off Highway 50. Boat ramp, boat rentals, picnic area, fire pits, and restroom and parking facilities.

PICNIC AREAS. *Truckee River Park.* Off Highway 50, just over the Upper Truckee River (adjacent to Carrows Restaurant). Picnic tables, and fishing; no other facilities.

Taylor Creek. At the mouth of the creek; approach via trail from the Visitors Center. No facilities apart from those available at the Visitors Center.

Fallen Leaf Lake. At the southern end of the lake; from Highway 89 turn into Fallen Leaf Road and follow south. In addition to a picnic area, a small beach, restrooms, a coffee shop and marina are also available.

Bayview Picnic Area. Just off Highway 89, at the southwest corner of Emerald Bay. Facilities include picnic tables, fire pits and restrooms.

Inspiration Point. On Highway 89, above the Bayview Picnic Area. Picnicking, and restrooms.

Eagle Falls. On Highway 89, at the head of Emerald Bay. Picnic area, fire pits, restrooms.

Emerald Bay Picnic Area. Near Vikingsholm, on the Emerald Bay shore. Small beach area, picnicking, and restrooms; parking off Highway 89. Camping available in summer.

D.L. Bliss State Park. Off Highway 89, north of Emerald Bay; look for sign. Picnic area, campsites, fire pits, restrooms, and parking; dogs on leash only.

CAMPGROUNDS. With nearly 2000 campsites in over a dozen campgrounds scattered in and around the South Tahoe area, you never have to travel a great distance to find some place to camp out. Most of these camping facilities, however, are open only from Memorial Day until late fall; only a few remain open all year.

D.L. Bliss Campground. Alongside Highway 89, north of Emerald Bay. 168 sites, restrooms, swimming, hiking and fishing; 10-day limit. Reservations (916) 525-7277.

Emerald Bay Campground. On the north shore of Emerald Bay, off Highway 89. 20 sites, restrooms, swimming and fishing; 10-day limit. Phone (916) 541-3030.

Eagle Point Campground. Near the mouth of Emerald Bay, on the southeast corner (entrance off Highway 89, 4½ miles northwest of Camp Richardson). 100 sites, restrooms, showers, swimming, hiking and fishing; 10-

day limit. Reservations (916) 541-3030.

Fallen Leaf Campground. Just north of Fallen Leaf Lake, ½ mile in from the highway (89). 205 sites, restrooms, swimming, fishing, hiking and riding; 7-day limit. Phone (916) 544-6420.

Fallen Leaf Lodge Campground. At the end of Fallen Leaf Road, on the southern tip of Fallen Leaf Lake. 37 sites, restrooms, showers, boat ramp, store, laundromat, swimming, hiking and fishing; no pets. No day limit. Reservations (916) 541-3366.

Camp Richardson. On Highway 89, 1½ miles northwest of South Lake Tahoe. 230 sites, restrooms, showers, electrical hook-ups, store, laundromat, marina and stables; no pets. No day limit. Reservations (916) 541-1801.

Tahoe Valley Recreation Camp. Off Highway 50, just west of the South Tahoe Y. 300 sites, restrooms, showers, electrical hook-ups, store, hiking; no day limit. Open year-round. Reservations (916) 541-2222.

Tahoe Pines Campground. On Highway 50, in Tahoe Paradise. 60 sites, restrooms, showers, electrical hook-ups, hiking, riding and fishing; no day limit. Open all year. Reservations (916) 577-1653.

KOA Campground. Highway 50, Tahoe Paradise. 20 sites, restrooms, showers, electrical hook-ups, store, laundromat, swimming, hiking, riding and fishing; no day limit. Open year-round. Reservations (916) 577-3693.

El Dorado Campground. Situated in the city area, at the corner of Rufus Allen and Lake Tahoe Boulevard (Highway 50). 166 sites, restrooms, showers, electrical hook-ups, boat ramp, recreation and beach area, swimming and fishing; 15-day limit. Reservations (916) 544-3317.

Nevada Beach Campground. Off Highway 50 east, 1 mile north of the Stateline casinos. 54 sites, restrooms, store, laundromat, swimming and fishing; 7-day limit. Reservations (916) 544-6420.

Zephyr Cove Resort Campground. Highway 50 east, 4 miles north of the Stateline. 170 sites, restrooms, showers, electrical hook-ups, boat ramp, store, laundromat, beach area, swimming and fishing; 14-day limit. Open all year. Reservations (702) 588-6644.

Outlying-area campgrounds, mostly situated 8-10 miles southwest of Tahoe Paradise (Meyers), include: *Crystal Springs,* 21 sites, (702) 882-2766; *Hope Valley,* 20 sites, (702) 882-2766; *Kit Carson,* 12 sites, (702) 882-2766; *Snowshoe Springs,* 13 sites, (702) 882-2766; *Grover Hot Springs,* 76 sites, (916) 694-2248; *Indian Creek Reservoir,* 29 sites, (702) 882-1631; and *Markleeville Campground,* 10 sites, (702) 882-2766.

MARINAS. There are six marinas on the south shore, most of them fully equipped with boats, water-skis, sail-boards and other water sports equipment rentals, sales and service.

Richardson's Marina. Off Highway 89, on Jameson Beach Road, Camp Richardson. Facilities available: buoys, ramp, hoist, rentals, gas supplies, and repair service. Open all year. Phone (916) 541-1777.

Tahoe Keys Marina. Off Tahoe Keys Boulevard, on Venice Drive, Tahoe Keys. 150 slips, ramp, forklift launching, rentals, gas supplies, repair service, sales and storage. Open year-round. Phone (916) 541-2155.

Timber Cove Marina. Off Highway 50, on Wagon Road, Bijou (behind Timber Cove Lodge). Buoys, hoist, rentals, gas supplies, repair, service and sales. Open through summer. Phone (916) 544-2942.

Ski Run Marina. At the lake's end of Ski Run Boulevard, in the city. 35 slips, buoys, ramp, gas supplies, repairs, rentals, sales, beach and snack bar. Open summers. Phone (916) 544-0200.

Lakeside Marina. At the bottom of Park Avenue, near Stateline. 94 slips, buoys, ramp, gas supplies, rentals, sales and storage. Open summers. Phone (916) 541-6626.

Zephyr Cove Marina. Off Highway 50 east, 4 miles north of the Stateline. Buoys, ramp, rentals, supplies, and restaurant. Open through summer. Phone (702) 588-3833.

Public Launching Ramps. There are five: at *El Dorado Beach,* in the city area; at *Zephyr Cove,* north from the Stateline; at *Cave Rock,* 3 miles north of Zephyr Cove; at *Logan Shoals,* 1½ miles north of Cave Rock (just off Highway 50); and at *Glenbrook,* farther north.

GOLF. As anywhere else, golf is an ever-popular, established sport at South Lake Tahoe. The area has five courses, with extensive facilities and a variety in terrain; lessons are available at most.

Tahoe Paradise Golf Course. Off Highway 50, 4 miles south of the Y. 18 holes, 4119 yards, 66 Par; Green Fee: $18.50/18 Holes, $11.00/9 Holes. Facilities: Carts, pro shop, driving range, coffee shop. For enquiries, call (916) 577-2121.

Lake Tahoe Country Club. 1 mile south of the Lake Tahoe Airport, on Highway 50. 18 holes, 6588 yards, 71 Par; Green Fee: $23.00/18 Holes. Carts, pro shop, driving range, cocktail lounge and snack bar. Enquiries: (916) 577-0788.

Bijou Golf Course. Wedged between Johnson Boulevard and Fairway Avenue, in the city. 9 holes, 2015 yards, 33 Par; Green Fee: $4.00/9 holes. Carts. Enquiries: (916) 544-5500.

Edgewood Tahoe Golf Club. On Loop Road, behind the High Sierra Hotel-Casino. 18 holes, 7563 yard championship course, 72 Par; Green Fee: $75.00/with cart (cart mandatory). Pro shop, driving range, restaurant, bar. Enquiries: (702) 588-3566.

Glenbrook Golf Course. On the east shore, 8 miles north of the Stateline. 9 holes, 2591 yards, 34 Par; green fees. Carts, pro shop, driving range, bar and snack bar. Enquiries: (702) 749-5201.

TENNIS. For tennis enthusiasts, the south shore offers three different tennis court locations:

South Tahoe High School. Lake Tahoe Boulevard, 1 mile west of the Tahoe Valley Y. 6 courts, lights. Reservations (916) 541-4611.

South Tahoe Intermediate School. Lyons Avenue, off Lake Tahoe Boulevard (Highway 50). 8 courts, lights. Reservations (916) 541-4611.

George Whittle High School. Warrior Way, Zephyr Cove (off Highway 50 east). 4 courts, lights. Reservations (702) 588-3666.

HORSEBACK RIDING. Riding horseback through South Tahoe's back-country is an experience quite unlike any other — relaxed, refreshing and soul-searching. And catering to this recreational activity are five fully-stocked stables, offering both rentals and a variety of trail rides (with or without a guide), scenic pleasure rides, hay rides, buggy rides, wagon rides, sleigh rides, breakfast, lunch and sunset rides, hunting and pack trips, cross-country courses, and even lessons. For detailed information, contact any of these stables: *Camp Richardson Corral,* 2½ miles northwest of the Tahoe Valley Y, on Emerald Bay Road, (916) 541-3113; *Cascade Stables,* 1¼ miles past Camp Richardson, also on Emerald Bay Road, (916) 541-2055; *Stateline Stables*, Park Avenue (behind the

Crescent V Shopping Center), next to the Stateline, (916) 541-0962; *Tahoe Equestrian Center;* ½ mile south of the Lake Tahoe Airport on Highway 50, (916) 541-9944; *Zephyr Cove Riding Stables,* 4½ miles north of the Stateline casinos (at Zephyr Cove Resort), (702) 588-6136.

 WINTER SPORTS. South Tahoe enjoys an annual snowfall of approximately 300 inches, with average winter temperatures in the 25-30°F range — ideal for skiing, snowmobiling, tobogganing, or just plain snow fun.

Downhill Ski Areas. *Heavenly Valley.* This 20-square-mile expanse, America's largest alpine ski area, straddles the California-Nevada stateline a couple of miles to the south of South Lake Tahoe's "casino district"; West Heavenly lies in California, and Heavenly North in Nevada. In California, approach via Ski Run Boulevard, off Highway 50; in Nevada, Benjamin Drive, off the Kingsbury Grade, leads straight to the base of the mountain. Heavenly's elevations: top 10,167 feet, base 6,100 feet; vertical drop 3,600 feet. Facilities available: 26 lifts, helicopter skiing, NASTAR races, lessons, rentals, restaurant and bar, and shuttle bus. Lift prices: $27.00/adults, $13.00/children; half day: $19.00 adults, $13.00/children. Phone (916) 541-1330.

Kirkwood Ski Resort. Take Highway 89 south to Pickett's Junction; at the junction take Highway 88 west to Kirkwood. Although slightly out of the way, this ski area enjoys some of the heaviest snowfall in the region, and remains open through to the Fourth of July. Elevations: top 9,800 feet, base 7,800 feet; vertical drop 2,000 feet. Facilities include 9 lifts, NASTAR races, lessons, rentals, bar, snack bar, restaurant, store, and shuttle bus. Lift prices: $25.00/adults, $10.00/children; half day: $18.00/adults, $7.00/children. Phone (209) 258-6000.

Echo Summit. On Highway 50, 9 miles southwest of South Lake Tahoe. Elevations: top 7,950 feet, base 7,400 feet; vertical drop 550 feet. Facilities: 3 lifts, NASTAR races, lessons, rentals, and restaurant. Lift prices: $15.00/adult, $9.00/children; half day: $12.00/adult, $8.00/children. Phone (916) 659-7154.

Sierra Ski Ranch. Just off Highway 50, 12½ miles southwest of South Lake Tahoe. Elevations: top 8,852 feet, base 6,640 feet; vertical drop 2,212 feet. Facilities: 9 lifts, lessons, rentals, day lodges, snack bar, mountain top restaurant, and shuttle bus. Lift prices: $21.00/adults, $12.00/children; half day: $15.00/adults, $8.00/children. Phone (916) 659-7475.

Nordic Ski Areas. *Aschi Sports Cross Country.* Located at 3339 Highway 50, South Lake Tahoe (across from the Bank of America). 15 miles of trails, and tours, lessons and rentals are available. Trail fee: $3.00. Phone (916) 544-7873.

Echo Summit Nordic Center. South of South Lake Tahoe; at the Echo Summit Ski Area on Highway 50. 56 miles of trails; tours, lessons, rentals, restaurant, and child care facilities. Trail fee: $5.00. Phone (916) 659-7154.

Kirkwood Touring Center. At the Kirkwood Ski Area on Highway 88, 28 miles south of South Lake Tahoe. 70 miles of trails; tours, lessons, rentals, restaurant, lodge, child care, and shuttle bus. Trail fee: $10.00. Phone (209) 258-6000.

Strawberry Ski Touring. 14 miles from South Lake Tahoe on Highway 50 at Kyburz. 12 miles of trails; lessons, rentals, lodge. No trail fee. Phone (916) 659-7585.

Telemark Country Sports. On Highway 50, 4 miles south of South Lake Tahoe. 5 miles of trails; tours, lessons, rentals, and lodging facilities. Trail fee: $3.00. Phone (916) 577-6811.

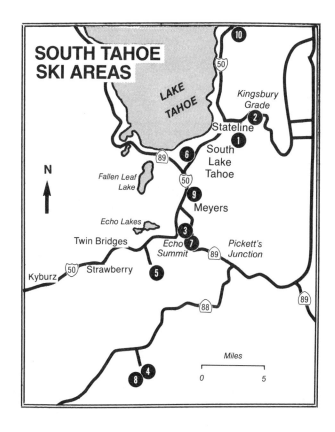

Downhill Ski Areas –
1) Heavenly Valley West
2) Heavenly Valley North
3) Echo Summit
4) Kirkwood Ski Resort
5) Sierra Ski Ranch

Nordic Ski Areas –
6) Aschi Sports
7) Echo Summit Nordic Center
8) Kirkwood Touring Center
9) Telemark Country Sports
10) Spooner Summit Nordic (Wilderness) Ski Area

Wilderness Cross-Country Ski Areas. There are several cross-country ski areas scattered in South Tahoe's State Parks and National Forest lands; contact the Forest Service for complete information. Among the popular areas, however, are the following:

Angora Ridge Area. Approach via Lake Tahoe Boulevard (west of the "Y") and Tahoe Mountain Road; the trailhead is situated just past Glenmore Way and Dundee Circle.

Tahoe Paradise Area. From Highway 50 (in the Tahoe Paradise area) turn into Pioneer Trail, then continue on down, about a mile, to Oneidas Street. The trailhead is just south of Oneidas, off Chibcha Street.

High Meadows Area. Take Pioneer Trail to High Meadows Trail, just south of Lake Christopher. Follow High Meadows Trail to the trailhead.

Toiyabe National Forest Area. Take the Kingsbury Grade (Route 207) to North Benjamin Drive, then follow North Benjamin to Andria Drive; the trailhead is located at the end of Andria Drive.

Spooner Summit Area. The trailhead is located near Spooner Summit, just east of the junction of Highways 50 and 28.

Snowmobiling. There are two locations, both in the Tahoe Paradise area, where groomed tracks are available for snowmobiling: *Lake Tahoe Country Club,* a mile south of the Lake Tahoe Airport on Highway 50, (916) 577-0788; and *Tahoe Paradise Snowmobiling* at Tahoe Paradise, just off Highway 50, (916) 577-2121. Guided back-country tours are available with *Alpine Limousine and Tour Company,* South Lake Tahoe (916) 577-2727.

Snow Play Areas. There are a couple of snow play areas on the south shore; one is located just north of Taylor Creek, while the other, *Hansen's Resort,* is situated off Ski Run Boulevard in the city. Hansen's offers on-site equipment, banked turns and packed runs, mechanical lift returns, and even lodging on the premises.

 CASINOS. South Lake Tahoe has one of the finest casino districts in the country, with Las Vegas style casinos. Gambling is offered around the clock, with the variety ranging from basic slot machines to craps, keno, blackjack, poker, roulette, and even betting on horse races and ball games. The casinos also offer some of the best in big name entertainment, booking country singers, comedians, entertainers, and headliner stars of every description. The hotel rooms at the clubs are well-appointed, and some delightful restaurants can be found there too. There are some 24-hour coffee shops and snack bars worth visiting here as well, especially between midnight and 6 a.m. when one can enjoy $1.99 ham and eggs breakfasts.

If you are staying at a motel in town, ask about the casino-sponsored courtesy buses between your motel and the casinos. Most motels, in conjunction with the casinos, also offer "casino fun packages" which usually comprise a small dollar amount in nickels or dimes to get you started on the slots.

Harvey's Resort Hotel is the oldest club on the block, propped right up at the California-Nevada stateline. It was originally built in 1960, comprising 11 stories and 200 rooms and claiming the distinction of being the first highrise at Lake Tahoe. In 1986, a new 22-story, 547-room wing was added to the hotel. The hotel boasts a lovely decor, featuring suede-clothed walls, granite pillars and oak and brass accents. There is also a glass elevator of considerable interest here, which climbs from the casino floor to the *Top of the Wheel* restaurant, offering some splendid views of the lake and the Sierra along the way. The *Top of the Wheel* also offers marvelous views, as well as live entertainment, late evening dancing and some of the finest in

Polynesian dining. Harvey's has six other restaurants as well, all quite good. Visit also the *Casino Theater Lounge* for live entertainment. For show information and reservations, call (702) 588-2411.

Harrah's Tahoe boasts 18 stories and 540 rooms, originally built in 1973. It is located directly across from Harvey's, with part of its large parking lot spilling over onto the California side of the stateline. Harrah's has a 70,000-square-foot casino with 190 games and 2200 slot machines. Of interest too are the hotel's *South Shore Room* and the *Stateline Cabaret,* where live entertainment can be enjoyed. Visit also *The Summit* restaurant and lounge, perched on the 18th floor, offering spectacular views of Lake Tahoe, and great gourmet cuisine. There is a worthwhile shopping arcade here as well. For information on shows, call (702) 588-6611 locally, or (800) 648-3773 from California.

Caesar's Tahoe, situated a hundred yards or so east of Harrah's, is part of the famous Caesar's Palace, Las Vegas chain. It has 15 stories, 446 guest rooms and a rambling shopping arcade. There are also six delightful restaurants here, including *Edgewood,* billed as "one of the most elegant restaurants in Northern Nevada." For live entertainment visit the *Cascade Showroom,* or the *Caesar's Comedy Corner.* For reservations and show information, call (702) 588-3515 in Nevada, and (800) 648-3353 from out of state.

The High Sierra. Formerly the Sahara Tahoe, this 14-story hotel-casino was built in 1965. It stands almost directly opposite Caesar's, with a side entrance off Loop Road. The name change occurred in 1983, at which time it was also redecorated in Old West splendor; even its employees now sport cowboy hats and velvety waistcoats. The hotel has five notable restaurants, with live entertainment featured at the *Pine Cone Lounge* and nightly dancing at *Lily's Dance Hall.* For show reservations, call (702) 588-6211, or (800) 648-3322.

Barney's. This is the smallest club on the block, wedged between Caesar's and Harrah's. It bills itself "the cozy little club." There is a cocktail lounge and coffee shop here, and two floors of casino games. Phone (702) 588-2455.

John's Tahoe Nugget. Located just past the Kingsbury Grade turnoff, this is not a large club, but nevertheless quite popular. Visit the club's *Stagecoach Bar* for live entertainment. Show information and reservations: (702) 588-6288.

 DINING OUT. With well over 100 restaurants to choose from, South Lake Tahoe has something for every palate: Gourmet, Continental, French, Italian, American, Mexican and Oriental cuisine; even pizza parlors and fast-food outlets are plentiful in the area.

Restaurant prices — on the basis of full course dinner, excluding drinks, tax and tips — are categorized as follows: *Deluxe,* over $25; *Expensive,* $15-$25; *Moderate,* $10-$15; *Inexpensive,* under $10.

Gourmet

The Summit. *Deluxe.* At Harrah's Hotel-Casino. Views are spectacular from its 18th floor vantage point; also some memorable continental cuisine. Live music. Reservations (702) 588-6606.

Christiania Inn. *Deluxe.* Across from Heavenly Valley Ski Area. Delightful alpine setting and casual fireside elegance; dining room featured in *Bon Appetit* magazine. Creative desserts. Also some accommodations. Reservations (916) 544-7337.

Edgewood. *Deluxe*. At Caesar's Casino-Hotel. Noted as one of Northern Nevada's most elegant restaurants; Chateaubriand specialty. Reservations (702) 588-3575.

The Sage Room. *Expensive*. At Harvey's Resort Hotel, Stateline. Exceptional dining, with several dishes prepared at the tableside. Reservations (702) 588-2411.

The Hearthside. *Expensive*. On Saddle Road, across from the Heavenly ski area. Famous for its Sunday Mimosa Brunches on Sunday mornings, with champagne, cheeses, smoked salmon, omelettes, salads and pastries. Phone (916) 541-6700.

Steaks and Seafood

Stetson. *Deluxe*. At the High Sierra Hotel-Casino. Reservations (702) 588-6211.

Friday's Station. *Expensive*. At Harrah's, Stateline. Reservations (702) 588-6606.

Sea Cove. *Expensive*. At Harrah's. Reservations (702) 588-6606.

Zachary's. *Expensive*. Behind Roundhill Mall, 2 miles north of Stateline. Reservations (702) 588-2108.

The Dory's Oar. *Expensive*. 1041 Fremont Avenue, South Lake Tahoe. Established in 1975. New England setting, with Maryland soft shell crabs a specialty. Phone (916) 541-6603.

Hodges. *Expensive*. On Highway 50, near Ski Run Blvd. Garden style restaurant with delightful soup and salad bar. Phone (916) 541-6220.

Fresh Ketch. *Expensive*. At the Tahoe Keys Marina. Spectacular views of the lake, and an enchanting waterfall featured inside the restaurant. Long Island oysters a favorite; also some poultry. Reservations (916) 541-5683.

French

Chez Villaret. *Deluxe*. 536 Emerald Bay Road. Classic French selections and an award winning wine list. This is south shore's finest French restaurant. Phone (916) 541-7868.

Italian

Tep's Villa Roma. *Expensive*. Corner of Highway 50 and Reno Avenue, South Lake Tahoe. Traditional Italian dishes, and freshly baked garlic sticks and Italian breads. Phone (916) 541-8227.

Ristorante Tre Fontane. *Expensive*. On Highway 50, in Tahoe Paradise. Reservations (916) 577-2016.

Continental

Swiss Chalet. *Expensive*. 2450 Highway 50, South Lake Tahoe. Owned and operated by the chef for 29 years. Excellent steaks and European cuisine. Phone (916) 544-3304.

Cuckoo's Nest Cafe. *Expensive*. 2502 Highway 50, South Lake Tahoe. Phone (916) 541-0873.

Forest Room. *Moderate*. At Harrah's Hotel-Casino. Phone (702) 588-6606.

El Dorado Buffet. *Moderate*. At Harvey's Resort Hotel. Great buffet luncheons, ideal for family dining. Phone (702) 588-2411.

American

The Beacon. *Moderate*. Camp Richardson, Emerald Bay Road, South Lake Tahoe. Lakeside setting. Open for breakfast, lunch and dinner; also weekend brunch. Phone (916) 541-0630.

Chicken and Rib House. *Moderate*. At the High Sierra Casino-Hotel. Phone (702) 588-6211.

Condor Lodge. *Inexpensive*. 3838 Highway 50, South Lake Tahoe. Phone (916) 541-5400.

Womack's Texas Style Bar-B-Que. *Moderate*. 1169 Ski Run Boulevard, South Lake Tahoe. Phone (916) 541-9191.

Polynesian

Top of the Wheel. *Deluxe*. At Harvey's Resort Hotel. Panoramic views and live entertainment. A superb dining experience. Reservations (702) 588-2411.

Oriental

House of Woo. *Moderate*. At Caesar's Tahoe Hotel-Casino. Szechwan, Hunan, Cantonese and Mandarin cuisine. Phone (702) 588-3515.

Sushi House. *Moderate*. 3733 Highway 50, South Lake Tahoe. Phone (916) 542-1242.

The Waterwheel. *Moderate*. Crescent V Shopping Center, cnr. Hwy. 50 and Park Ave., South Lake Tahoe. Authentic Mardarin Szechwan cuisine. Phone (916) 544-4158.

Mexican

Cantino Los Tres Hombres. *Moderate*. Corner Highway 89 and 10th Street. Phone (916) 544-1233.

El Vacquero. *Moderate*. At Harvey's Resort Hotel. Phone (702) 588-2411.

Los Aguirres. *Inexpensive*. 2212 Lake Tahoe Boulevard, South Lake Tahoe. (916) 541-9849.

NORTH LAKE TAHOE

Wilderness and Summer Homes

North Lake Tahoe is a loosely defined, seasonally inhabited area, with roughly 40 miles of shoreline and completely surrounded by two of the most splendid forests — the Tahoe National Forest and the Toiyabe National Forest. There are at least one-half dozen state parks here as well, and several drives and walks through gorgeous, thickly-wooded back-country.

There are three broad geographic divisions of North Lake Tahoe: the West Shore, the North Shore, and the Tahoe-Truckee Route area (essentially the Truckee River Canyon area). The north and west shores are made up largely of tiny resort communities, dotted with hundreds of vacation homes, and with few year-round residents. Most of the permanent population of the area is concentrated mainly in four centers — Tahoe City, Kings Beach-Crystal Bay, Incline Village and Truckee — all of which are linked together via four or five state highways. Truckee, for instance, is linked to Tahoe City via Highway 89; Kings Beach and Crystal Bay are linked to Truckee by way of Highway 267; Incline Village, Kings Beach and Tahoe City are linked by Highway 28 (with Route 431 linking Incline to Highway 395 which leads to Reno); and the west shore communities are strung together and linked to Tahoe City by 89 south.

North Lake Tahoe is accessible by way of Interstate 80, which passes just over Truckee and intersects with a couple of the highways feeding into the North Tahoe area. There is also a non-commercial airport, the Tahoe-Truckee Airport, just to the southeast of Truckee.

THE TAHOE-TRUCKEE ROUTE

The Tahoe-Truckee Route comprises mainly the townships of Truckee and Tahoe City, lying some 15 miles apart, and the resort communities of Alpine Meadows and Squaw Valley which are just to the northwest of Tahoe City. The route follows the Truckee River through an ancient canyon formed thousands of years ago by an off-shoot glacier. It is especially picturesque in spring, when the river flows heartily, fuller with the snowmelt, its banks awash with light-green brush and a sprinkling of native wildflowers.

The Tahoe-Truckee Route is among the earliest incursions into North Lake Tahoe, dating from the late 1850's when the "Tahoe-Truckee Toll Road," a dusty, rutted turnpike, barely the width of a stagecoach, passed through the canyon. Several early day personages traveled by way of it, including Generals Ulysses S. Grant and Philip H. Sheridan, and the British royal mistress, Lily Langtree. In 1900 even a narrow-gauge railroad was pushed through the canyon, the first ever passenger train to enter the Lake Tahoe Basin; it provided rail service between Tahoe City and Truckee for over one-quarter of a century.

Today the route continues to forge a vital link between two of North Tahoe's most important towns. The present highway (Highway 89), however, is cut at a slightly higher elevation than the original tollroad, but a bicycle path below the highway and closer to the river offers some unique opportunities and a slower pace by which to explore.

Truckee

The town of Truckee lies to the northwest of Tahoe City at the intersection of Interstate 80 and Highways 89 and 267, posing as both a crossroads and a "gateway" to North Lake Tahoe. Truckee is notable mostly for its historic inheritance, never more apparent than in its "historic downtown." Covered wooden walkways protrude from clapboard store-fronts, reminiscent of the Old West, and of some 300 buildings nestled there, nearly a third date from the 19th century and more than half from before World War II. Most of the buildings, however, are currently in use, housing specialty shops, restaurants and hotels. On Commercial Row, Truckee's main street, are the Oak and Brass Shoppe, which is the third oldest building in town, and the old I.O.O.F. Hall which was built by the Oddfellows in 1871 and where the I.O.O.F. still occupies the upper floor, with a delicatessen at ground level; the Oak & Brass Shoppe was originally built as a saloon in 1870, and among the shop's many fixtures is an antique back bar that once belonged in an historic Virginia City saloon. A few doors down, outside Cabona's, another store on Commercial Row, is a plaque commemorating an early day vigilante group, "the 601." On the south side of the street is to be found the Southern Pacific Railroad Depot,

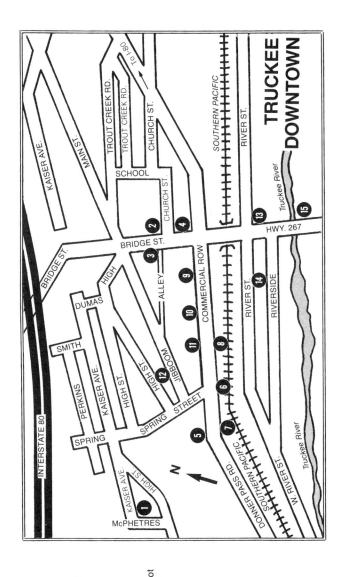

Points of Interest –
1) Rocking Stone Tower
2) Gray's Log Cabin
3) Alpenglow
4) Truckee Hotel
5) C.B. White's
6) Loading Dock
7) Ice House
8) Southern Pacific Depot
9) Oak & Brass Shoppe
10) I.O.O.F. Hall
11) The "601" Plaque
12) Truckee Jailhouse
13) La Vieille Maison
14) Star Hotel
15) Chinese Herb Shop

dating from 1896 (although the first trans-Sierra crossing occurred in April, 1868), an inerasable reminder of Truckee's humble beginnings as a railroad settlement. Farther along from the depot are the old Ice House and the Loading Dock, both charming 19th century structures.

There are two Victorian buildings located on Commercial Row too: C.B. White's restaurant, a Queen Anne Victorian with distinctive white-lace trim, built in 1874 by an early day lumber mill owner, W.H. Kruger, and later, in 1903, bought by an eminent banker, C.B. White, for whom it is named; and the Truckee Hotel (circa 1871), an unclassified Victorian, boasting 42 guest rooms decorated in 19th century splendor. The hotel, in fact, fronts on Bridge Street, and has a restaurant of considerable repute, The Passage, where live music is featured most evenings. Adjacent to the Truckee Hotel, just north of Church Street, is Truckee's oldest building, Gray's Log Cabin, built in 1863 by Joseph Gray, the town's first white settler. The cabin originally stood across the street from its present location, where the Alpenglow sports store now stands, but was moved in 1903. The stone structure of Alpenglow is also not without historic merit; it was built in 1907, as a carriage house and blacksmith shop.

Also of interest is Jibboom Street (which runs at an angle at the back of Commercial Row), once the town's "red light district," sporting dozens of saloons and brothels. Upon it is now to be seen the old Truckee Jail, built in 1875 and said to be one of the West's oldest "town jails"; the jail was operative until 1964. Take the time also to drive up Spring Street, at the top end of which is to be found the Rocking Stone Tower where a 17-ton rock balances precariously on its natural rock pedestal, known to be one of only 25 such rocks in the world. Recently the "rocking stone" was cemented to its base to prevent any accidents, but even so the rocking motion has not been completely lost. Legend has it that the Washoe Indians used the rock's rocking motion to grind nuts and seeds in the early days.

Over the railroad tracks on the south side of Commercial Row, flanking Highway 267, are to be found the La Vieille Maison and the Star Hotel. The "maison" was built in 1885 as a boarding house for lumberjacks and railroad and ice workers, and the hotel was built in 1869, also as a boarding house, by George Schaffer, contemporary and partner of Joseph Gray. Just south of La Vieille Maison is the old Chinese Herb Shop, a brick building with double iron doors, built in 1878. This is especially interesting for it is perhaps the last reminder of Truckee's once thriving Chinese community of some 10,000 strong. Truckee's Chinatown in fact was the second largest in the West during the 1860's and the only one if its kind in the High Sierra. But racial hatred plagued the Chinese, and by 1886 not a single Chinaman remained in Truckee. The legacy of the Chinese, however, lingers to this day, for they, more than anyone else, had provided the labor for the building of the Central Pacific Railroad over the Sierra.

South on Highway 267 lies Martis Valley, with a lake of the same name nearby. In the valley are to be found the Tahoe-Truckee Airport, North Tahoe's only airport, and an elaborate sewage plant, billed as "the most modern tertiary plant in the world," through which the Tahoe-Truckee Sanitation Agency conducts year-round tours. At the airport a couple of local aviation companies offer scenic flights over the lake, and in June the Truckee Airshow gets underway there, providing for some thrilling aerobatics and displays of vintage airplanes. In winter the airport hosts the annual Sled Dog Races.

Four miles to the west of Truckee's downtown, on Donner Pass Road, which is really an extension of Commercial Row, one arrives at the Donner Memorial State Park, named for the ill-fated Donner Party who are believed to have camped here during the fateful winter of 1846-47. According to history, the emigrant party led by George Donner became lost in these parts while attempting to cross over the Sierra. The party was ill-prepared for the bitter conditions they encountered, and eventually food in the camp ran out. Several members of the party perished as hunger and the cold gripped them, and the survivors resorted to cannibalism to stay alive until they were found by a rescue party the following spring. Of the original party of 89, 42 are said to have perished. In the park stands a monument, the Emigrant Monument, commemorating the tragedy; the statue of a "Donner family" stands atop a 22-foot high pedestal, the height of the pedestal ironically indicating the depth of the snow during that perilous winter. Nearby, the one and one-half mile long and half-mile wide Donner Lake, too, is named for the party. There is an Emigrant Museum not far from the monument, displaying several artifacts and old photographs recounting the Donner Party story and the Central Pacific Railroad days. A sports museum, the Western American Ski Sport Museum, is located farther on at Soda Springs, accessible from I-80; here are to be found early day ski exhibits, some of them dating from 1860, as well as some Squaw Valley Winter Olympic Games memorabilia. Also to be recommended is a drive along the old Highway 40, which runs parallel to I-80; scenic views present themselves enroute, together with some rare glimpses of railroad "snow-sheds" constructed in the Central Pacific Railroad days, more than a century ago.

Truckee is also notable for its many lakes and reservoirs, among them Donner Lake and the Boca, Prosser and Stampede reservoirs. While producing excellent quantums of trout, these lakes and reservoirs are all the more interesting for their part in Truckee's "ice industry," the most unusual industry the town has ever known. Between 1870 and 1927, ice was commercially "harvested" here and transported to far away markets on board the railroad, which by then had become central to Truckee's prosperity. Horses with spiked shoes were employed to drag across plows, skimming off snow from the ice, then cutters were drawn through the ice, again with the use of horses, to cut the ice into convenient slabs measuring 18 feet by 36 feet. The storage of the ice was a marvel in itself, with slabs stacked one on top of another, in rows alternately vertical and horizontal, and insulated with sawdust; it is told that when one such ice-storage unit burned down at the turn of the century, it took nearly three years for the ice in it to melt, so tightly was it packed.

Apart from the historic aspect, there is much else that Truckee boasts. In fact, this is one of the fastest growing communities on the northern part of the lake today, with a host of modern shops, shopping centers, restaurants, lodging facilities, campgrounds, two golf courses, an elementary school, a high school, judicial courts, a local theater group, and even a local newspaper, the *Sierra Sun*. Coupled with this is the town's envious position of being only minutes away from several of North Lake Tahoe's ski areas, both alpine and nordic.

Some local events, such as the "Bath Tub Races" at Donner Lake and the Truckee Rodeo at the Truckee River Park, add even more color. A striking fact about this robust little town, however, is that it is known to record some of the coldest temperatures in the state, but that, Truckee residents will tell you, is an added attraction for most Californians who have known only the sunny coastline. Indeed, here is a mountain town, at once historic and vital, with Reno, "the Las Vegas of Northern Nevada," only 34 miles away.

South To Squaw Valley and Alpine Meadows

The drive south from Truckee on Highway 89 is most enchanting, with the Truckee River flowing alongside of the road and lush pine forests creeping up the granite walls of the canyon. Some 8 miles south, on the east side of the highway, the twin peaks, Big Chief and Little Chief (elevations 7232 and 7255 feet, respectively), come into view. Big Chief is the more notable of the two, its west face vaguely resembling the profile of an Indian Chief, for which it is named. And like most other interesting-looking peaks and rocks in the region, this, too, has been romanticized by a Washoe Indian legend which traces the origins of the profile. According to the legend there once dwelled an Indian tribe just east of the peak here, and the chief of the tribe had a beautiful daughter named Cedar Heart. The chief was overly protective and even jealous of his daughter. He would not allow her to marry among the tribe's braves, nor would he let her be seen with the young warriors of the tribe. But one day, as the story goes, the chief found Cedar Heart with a young brave named Ko-ta-ki. This enraged the chief and he sought to have Ko-ta-ki put to death. But the couple fled, and the chief assembled a war party and followed. The pursuit wound down to the edge of the precipice where the Big Chief profile is now to be seen. Here the young lovers saw the angry chief and his war party not far behind, and they panicked; hand in hand they leaped to their deaths. The chief, upon seeing what he had done, sank to the ground, his face in the dirt, saddened, even deeply bereaved. Then a storm broke out, lasting several hours. When finally the storm subsided, the chief tried to rise but could not; his sorrow was too great, and the Great Spirit had frozen his body to the ground. Thus the big chief remained, as the rain and snow beat upon him, his body slowly disintegrating into the folds of the earth — but his face became embedded in the rock, and there it remains, looking out over what has come to be known as "Lover's Leap."

Below the Big Chief peak is a lodge of the same name, noted for its fine home-cooked meals. There are some summer rental cabins nearby, and across from the lodge many miles of groomed cross-country ski trails lead off into National Forest land.

Two miles to the southwest of Big Chief lies the internationally famed Squaw Valley, site of the VIII Winter Olympic Games in 1960. At the Squaw Valley Road turnoff is seen the five-ringed Olympic insignia, with the Olympic flame flickering above it. Most of the Olympic era landmarks, however, are gone from the scene. The old Olympic ice arena, Blythe Arena, which was quite a marvel in its time with an unconventional, outsized roof suspended from steel cables which were then affixed to heavy concrete beams on the outside, crumbled under the weight of the snow in 1983. Part of the old Olympic ski jump is still intact though, seen on the south side of the valley. Another point of interest is the Olympic Village Inn, a lovely alpine-design condominium complex, with one or two interesting restaurants, sprawled on the very site of the original Olympic Village where the athletes were housed and fed during the 1960 Games.

Squaw Valley is a natural amphitheater, surrounded by a series of noble mountain peaks, the highest of which, Granite Chief, soars 9050 feet, providing for some excellent skiing. The ski lodge area is nestled in the center of the bowl, with an aerial tram operating from the lodge to the Granite Chief restaurant some 2000 feet above; views from the tram are marvelous, mostly of the western Sierra and the lush meadows below, where horses can often be seen grazing in the summertime. Interestingly, the valley was the site of an elusive gold strike in the early 1860's, and later on a flourishing hay-farming community. It first opened to skiing in 1949, commanding the attention of the world in 1960. It now ranks among the world's leading alpine ski resorts, with roughly 100 ski trails, 27 ski lifts, including two gondolas, and hundreds of acres of skiable mountain. During "Snowfest" (a local winter festival held in early March) and over Christmas-New Year, Squaw Valley hosts some spectacular torch-light parades in which veteran skiers holding lighted torches descend the slopes in formation, creating a scene to behold.

Squaw Valley is also home to the illustrious. World class skiers Tamara McKinney and Melissa Dimino are intimately connected with the valley, having done much of their training on its slopes, and many of San Francisco's notables maintain vacation homes here. Writers Blair Fuller and Oakley Hall (author of *Warlock*) live here year-round, conducting a Writers' Workshop at the Squaw Valley Theater in the summer months, to which flock several distinguished writers, literary agents and publishers, as guest speakers.

Worth visiting at Squaw Valley too is Christy Hill, one of North Tahoe's finest restaurant-inns, and nearby on Squaw Valley Road is located a truly delightful delicatessen, Perkin's Pretty Good Grocery, boasting some great gourmet food selections. Several ski equipment and sporting goods stores are also to be found dotting Squaw Valley Road.

Receded back from the valley, just to the northwest, is the 40,000-acre, federally preserved Granite Chief Wilderness Area. A dozen or so hiking trails meander through it, some of them astonishingly scenic.

A mile south of Squaw Valley the highway crosses over onto the east side of the Truckee River and a little farther Alpine Meadows Road branches to the west, passing over a small bridge. At the turnoff here is to be found the much-talked-about River Ranch Inn and restaurant, where during the summer one can sit out on a large deck area facing south over the river and watch rafters slosh through the water at the end of their downriver ride, for this also serves as an egress point for many.

West of the River Ranch lies the nationally famous Alpine Meadows ski area, the scene of the "Anna Conrad Story"; it was here that the young ski patrol member survived an avalanche in 1982, buried

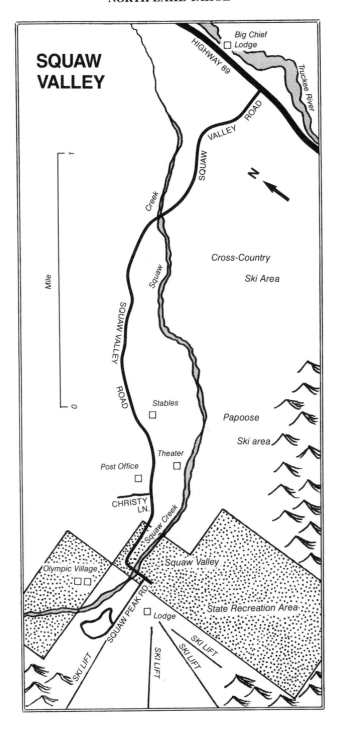

SQUAW VALLEY

Big Chief Lodge

HIGHWAY 89

Truckee River

SQUAW VALLEY ROAD

N

Creek

Cross-Country Ski Area

Squaw

Mile

1

0

SQUAW VALLEY ROAD

Stables

Papoose Ski area

Theater

Post Office

CHRISTY LN.

Squaw Creek

Olympic Village

Squaw Valley

State Recreation Area

Lodge

SQUAW PEAK RD.

SKI LIFT

SKI LIFT

SKI LIFT

beneath tons of snow for six whole days, a miracle that captivated much of the country. Alpine Meadows is nevertheless one of North Lake Tahoe's two biggest ski areas, second only to Squaw Valley, and boasts excellent ski conditions. There are over 2000 acres of skiable terrain here, and 100 different ski runs, including one that is two miles long. Alpine also enjoys an average annual snowfall of some 450 inches, and one of the longest ski seasons at the lake, remaining open well into spring, often until July 4. Much of the surrounding scenery is breathtaking, with lush, timbered mountains and the alpine peaks, Ward (elevation 8637 feet) and Scott (elevation 8246 feet), rising to the back of the meadows. Avid skiers will find the resort's NASTAR and other programs to be of particular interest; there is also a Handicap Ski School located here.

Tahoe City

Tahoe City is the oldest settlement of North Lake Tahoe, situated at the lake end of the Tahoe-Truckee Route. It is also the first lake resort to be christened "Tahoe" (the "city" was tacked on merely for grandeur in 1863 when the townsite was first surveyed and established). The town has a population of under 5,000, and only a dozen or so public streets, all told, ideally suited to exploring on foot. There is a charming little business district here, as well as some worthwhile historic buildings, all quite interesting to the visitor.

A place of special interest here, however, is the Fanny Bridge, located at the Tahoe City Y (intersection of Highways 89 and 28), especially attractive in summer. The bridge is built across the mouth of the Truckee River, the lake's sole outlet, and across from it are seen the historic Outlet Gates, comprising a dam built in 1910 to regulate the water flow from the lake. The outlet was first dammed in 1870, with a rock and timber crib, by one Colonel Von Schmidt, a controversial figure who once proposed to channel the lake's waters to San Francisco's bay area via a tunnel through the Sierra. There is a clear-water pool directly beneath the bridge, saturated with schools of Rainbow Trout, quite enjoyable to children. Worth visiting too is the Gatekeeper's (Log) Cabin, located near the southern end of the Outlet Gates. Originally built in the late 1800's to house the gatekeeper (custodian of the waters, in charge of releasing the waters), the cabin was recently renovated and now operates as the North Lake Tahoe Historical Society Museum, open in summer. There are several old photographs and artifacts depicting Lake Tahoe's past on display at the museum, as well as a collection of Tahoe greeting cards, hand-drawn and painted by local artists.

Also of historical interest is the Watson Log Cabin, located in the center of town, on the main street, North Lake Boulevard (Highway 28). The cabin was originally built in 1880 as the honeymoon cottage of Tahoe City pioneers, Robert and Stella Watson. It now houses the Potter's Wheel, an Indian rug and pottery store, with one or two quite impressive collections of genuine Navajo rugs. Directly across from the cabin stands the Big Tree, plumb in the center of the street, a Tahoe City landmark for nearly 120 years and now also the community Christmas Tree. On the lake side of the cabin the Tahoe City bluff

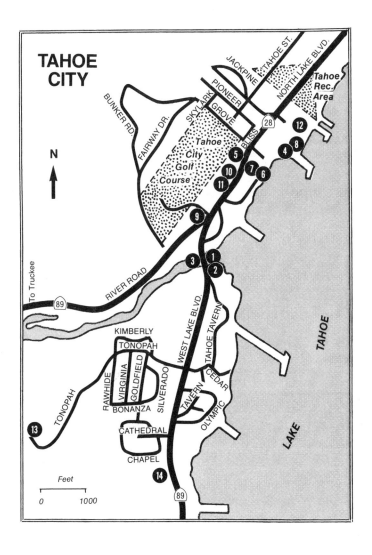

TAHOE CITY

N

TAHOE

LAKE

Places of Interest –

1) Lake Tahoe Dam
2) Gatekeeper's Cabin
3) Fanny Bridge
4) Roundhouse Mall
5) Big Tree
6) Tahoe Commons Beach
7) Watson Cabin

8) Tahoe City Boatworks
9) Tahoe City "Y"
10) Cobblestone Mall
11) Victoria Station
12) Lighthouse Center
13) Granlibakken
14) Stone Chapel

unfurls into a lovely, partially sanded and partially grassy area, known as the Tahoe City Commons. The recreation area was actually deeded to the people of Tahoe City several decades ago, hence the name "Commons." The Commons is also the site of the town's first wharf, built in 1864, and the scene of a famous gunfight (circa 1872) in which a local bartender shot and killed a notorious gunman, James Stewart, also known as the "Silent Terror." During the summer the beach area here is quite well liked, and on the Fourth of July all the townspeople gather here to watch the fireworks display.

Tahoe City also has some shopping malls of considerable interest. The Cobblestone Mall, located on North Lake Boulevard, is a charming replica of a Bavarian Alpine Village, with stucco walls, dark walnut trim, a Tudor mural on its feature wall, and a clock-faced turret above the north wing. Two others, the Boatworks Mall and the Roundhouse Mall, are farther to the east of Cobblestone, set slightly back from the highway. The Roundhouse Mall is actually housed in an old Southern Pacific Railroad building, dating from 1890, where a machine shop and a roundhouse were once to be found. There are some exquisite gift shops within and the Tahoe Boat Company Marina just at the front of the mall, where several antique boats can be seen during the Antique Boat Show in July. At the Boatworks Mall one can visit two or three splendid art galleries, as well as some specialty shops. Adjoining the Boatworks is the Lighthouse Center, with one chain shore, a bookstore and an array of interesting shops. The North Lake Tahoe Chamber of Commerce and the post office are also housed in the center.

Farther east from the malls, more or less on the eastern boundary of Tahoe City, is the Tahoe State Park Recreation Area, a triangular grassy tract with some picnicking facilities. And beyond, receded from the highway are the Tahoe City Judicial Courts, quite rustic and in a lovely forest setting.

Some of the other points of interest, just outside Tahoe City, include the site of the legendary Tahoe Tavern, an old, particularly charming stone chapel, and Lake Tahoe's oldest ski resort, Granlibakken, all located on West Lake Boulevard (Highway 89) just south of the Tahoe City Y. The Tahoe Tavern site has been built upon with the Tahoe Tavern Properties, a condominium development, on the east side of the highway. The Tavern is memorable mostly as the playground of the social sets from San Francisco and elsewhere during the 1920's and 1930's; it was then also considered to be one of the finest hotel-casinos at the lake. Built in 1901, the Tavern was razed in 1964. The Granlibakken Ski Resort is still in operation, however. It first opened to the public in 1926, boasting an "Olympic Hill" which comprised a ski jump and a toboggan run. Granlibakken (meaning "hillside sheltered by fir trees") is still the smallest ski area in the basin, though it now has a worthwhile lodge, and tennis courts for summer use. South from Granlibakken, also on the west side of the highway, is to be found Tahoe City's Episcopal Church, and a small but lovely stone chapel with tiny recessed windows, some with stained-glass, dating from 1909. The chapel is now the property of the Episcopal Church.

THE WEST SHORE

South from Tahoe City to the Rubicon Hills and the D.L. Bliss State Park, roughly 16 miles of shoreline and a dozen or so tiny, seasonally inhabited resort communities make up the west shore. This, then, is that wilderness country we have talked about, with lush, evergreen forests tumbling down the mountain sides to the very edge of the lake, with thickly wooded neighborhoods neatly tucked away into the bunched-up landscape, and with native brown bears to be seen every once in a while in late fall, ambling along on the outskirts of one of the higher, more remote subdivisions; often while motoring in these parts, usually on August mornings, one can even spot a coyote or two dashing across the road. The highway through here, Highway 89, is narrow and twisty, looping around granite protrusions and following closely a jagged shoreline; south from the Tahoe City "Y" to the Sugar Pine Point State Park it becomes the West Lake Boulevard, whereupon it turns into Emerald Bay Road until the D.L. Bliss State Park, continuing on south from there to the south shore communities. Several enchanting side streets branch off into the timbered neighborhoods and the abounding wilderness, providing for some delightful, secluded vistas. To the back of here rise at least nine different mountain peaks, each some 2000 feet above lake level, and six or seven unpretentious creeks meander on down to the lake, offering up good harvests of trout in spring. Then, too, there are two officially designated State Parks on the west shore, Sugar Pine Point and D.L. Bliss; a third, the Emerald Bay State Park, borders on the south side of the D.L. Bliss park. A great many well-wooded campgrounds and picnic areas are also to be found scattered throughout the area, with some lovely pebble beaches here and there.

The west shore is among the oldest of Lake Tahoe's vacation areas, where city folk came to sample the "wild" life of fishing and hunting as early as the 1870's. Thus, many of the area's earliest resorts, such as Sunnyside, Tahoe Pines, Homewood, Chamber's Landing, Sugar Pine Point and Meeks Bay, date back more than a century, with most of them still exhibiting a rural charm. And yet, creature comforts and modern resort facilities are to be found here just as readily as wilderness. There are four full-fledged marinas on the west shore, catering to a wealth of water activity, and three alpine ski areas — Homewood, Tahoe Ski Bowl and Granlibakken — grace the west shore mountains, all easily accessible from the highway. Many miles of groomed cross-country ski trails can also be enjoyed through the area's State Parks and National Forest lands, with a number of them substituting for hiking trails in the summertime; and 8 to 10 miles of bike paths follow alongside of the highway for a more peaceful look at the lake. Additionally, for lodging and dining out, some of the west shore's well-appointed lodges and European sounding restaurants can be quite comfortable. And "town" (Tahoe City), which is where west shore residents do much of their shopping, banking and socializing, is only a short drive to the north of here.

Sunnyside

Northernmost among west shore's resorts is Sunnyside, a pleasant little area situated above Ward Creek, just one and one-half miles south of Tahoe City. It is named for the bay upon which it sits and upon which the original "Sunnyside" cottage, pier and boathouse were built in the late 1800's. Central to Sunnyside is the Sunnyside Resort (and Marina) which now fronts on the bay. The resort building, recently remodelled, dates from 1907, originally built as the summer home of Captain Kendrick, a wealthy sea captain; the resort now also has a worthwhile restaurant. As for the marina snuggled up along the resort area — it first came to notice in 1925 when a group of affluent, amateur sailors from San Fransisco began congregating here, forming the prestigious Tahoe Yacht Club. It remains popular today with wealthy boat owners, who continue to moor their boats here.

The tract west of the Sunnyside Resort is known as Tahoe Park, with the Tahoe Park store fronting on the highway, close by the resort. Across from the store is a cluster of box-like cabins, housing the North Tahoe Fine Arts Council, and the Fire Sign Cafe where hot mulled wine can be leisurely sipped by a roaring fire in winter. The cafe is popular with west shore visitors, open for breakfast and lunch.

South of the resort lies the rectangle-shaped William Kent Campground, a favorite with summer vacationers, with a sandy beach spilling over onto the lake side of the highway. To the back of here is to be found the ruggedly beautiful Ward Canyon, arrived at by taking Wark Creek Boulevard, which is really a continuation of Pineland Drive, to the very end; the Twin Peaks (elevation 8878 ft.) are farther west from there. North of the canyon one can walk through the gently rolling Paige Meadows where native wildflowers are a main feature in summer; the meadows double as a cross-country ski area in winter. Also of interest, a short distance to the south of the William Kent campground, flows Ward Creek, upon which was built the west shore's first and only sawmill, Saxton's Mill, in 1864; the mill supplied railroad ties for the construction of Central Pacific's Sierra track in the mid 1860's.

South to Tahoe Pines

South of Sunnyside are three newer but nevertheless infinitely rustic neighborhoods, all with names ending in "land" — Pineland, Timberland and Skyland; Timberland, of course, is famous for those brown bear and coyote sightings. There are no shops or special attractions here, as such, though some of the small, wooded streets within are well worth driving down.

Some two miles after leaving Sunnyside, past the "lands," the highway curves around a shallow crescent with a pebble beach and a picnic area, known as the Kaspian Recreation Area. Immediately west of here, the much-talked-about Blackwood Canyon cuts deep into the hinterland, with a lovely tree-lined trail, by which to explore, passing through it. Almost directly ahead, perhaps a little to the north, the great Stanford Rock rises to a height of 8473 feet, and the Blackwood Creek meanders alongside, slowly filtering into the lake to the east. Quite like the Ward Canyon, Blackwood Canyon, too, is hiking country in summer and a cross-country ski area in winter, with snowmobiling as an added attraction. Some memorable snowmobile tours can be taken through here with one or the other of the local snowmobile rental operators (see section on *snowmobiling* in practical information).

Just around the corner from the Kaspian Recreation Area, where the highway leaves the shoreline, you'll see a naked twist of rock rise up above on the west side of the road, some 250 feet high. This is the legendary Eagle Rock, named for "White Eagle," an extraordinarily large eagle that soared above the rock long, long ago, and then one day turned into an Indian brave. Here is again a handed down Indian legend, according to which, the chief of the Washoe Indian tribe that dwelled here in the early times had a beautiful daughter who would not choose, for marriage, from among the braves of the tribe. In her solitude she would climb to the top of the rock and gaze out into the distance, hoping to perhaps see a handsome Indian warrior approaching. It was about that time that the great "White Eagle" began frequenting the rock, squawking as it soared above. The tribespeople knew not where the eagle had come from, but they soon grew to like it, and even looked upon it as a good omen. Then one day, as the story goes, the eagle left the rock, only to return a few days later with an arrow through its wing, and in great pain. The tribespeople saw what had happened and were deeply concerned. The Indian princess, the chief's daughter, ascended the rock and went over to the wounded eagle. There was pain and sadness in the bird's eyes. The princess carefully removed the arrow then bent over and kissed the eagle gently on its head. And instantly, to her utter amazement, the eagle turned into a handsome young brave. The Indian brave told the princess about an evil medicine man who had cast a spell on him, turning him into an eagle, to be turned back into a brave only if kissed by an Indian princess. Thus the couple remained a while, fell in love, came down from the rock, married, and lived happily ever after. Of course, the rock was also used as a lookout by the Washoe to watch the movements of their adversaries, the Paiute, and until the very early 1900's, Washoe Indians cleaned and dried fish beneath the rock, caught mostly from the adjoining Blackwood Creek, using forks and baskets.

The lakefront tract across from the rock, much of it heavily forested and therefore hidden from view, is known as Idlewild. This is where many of the west shore's wealthiest families maintain summer homes. In the 1890's, Idlewild became a renowned mecca of high society. Here the wealthy and the fashionable from San Francisco gathered, led by one Aimee Crocker Gillig Gouraud Miskinoff, so obviously boasting a collection of husbands, who went on to write the book, *I'd Do It Again*, followed by *Paula Loves Pearls* which was inspired by her excursion to the South Seas where, it is told, she made the "great sacrifice" to a South Seas Island chieftain in exchange for a beautiful black pearl. Today, however, Idlewild is a much more quiet, almost sleepy neighborhood.

Adjoining Idlewild on the south is one of the west shore's grandest and most famous privately-owned estates — "Fleur du Lac" — its noble, gray stone wall fronting on the highway for nearly one-quarter of a mile. This, in fact, is the former Henry J. Kaiser estate (Kaiser being the famous industrialist), originally built in 1939 in a record time of 29 days. Here were built six stone chalets, one for each of the top executives of "The Six Companies," around an elaborate mansion which became the summer home of Mr. and Mrs. Kaiser; here were also such illusory "mod cons" as a drive-in boat storage, an amphibious plane landing and an inland waterway. Later, in the 1970's, the movie *Godfather II,* was filmed on location at the estate. But much of what was, has been either demolished or "remodeled" since, and there now stands a cluster of multi-million dollar condominiums within those walls. In any case, "Fleur du Lac" is not open to the public, though you can always catch a glimpse or two of the estate's front structures and its rocked-in waterway and curious looking lighthouse by way of the lake. In summer, a cruise aboard North Tahoe Cruises' *Sunrunner* is to be recommended, for this pauses before the estate as part of its itinerary, and offers live commentary on the estate's history and other interesting features.

Opposite "Fleur du Lac," on the west side of the highway, an eye-catching, tri-colored sign reads, "Tahoe Pines, est. 1911," obviously taking great pride in the date. This, however, is Tahoe Pines, ranch country until the late 1870's. Here are to be found several older cabins, small but charming. And just south of here stands the Tahoe Swiss Village, quite in contrast with its large, expensive homes, most of them with views of the lake. Two or three magnificent, 1920's stone houses are seen here too.

Homewood

Homewood is a naturally sheltered resort settlement perched at the head of McKinney Bay, some two miles south of Tahoe Pines, and surrounded by a series of unclassified mountains. It is unique in that its alpine ski area and marina, namely the Homewood Ski Area and the High & Dry Marina, are separated by only some 20 feet of highway, the mere width of the road, (and if the mountain slopes were to have stretched another hundred yards or so farther, it is entirely possible that one could have taken a downhill as well as a water skiing lesson in one, single run). Homewood actually has two alpine ski areas and two marinas. The other ski area, Tahoe Ski Bowl, adjoins Homewood Ski on the south, sharing a ridge, the Rainbow Ridge, with the latter; here are some worthwhile beginners' slopes to be tested. The other marina, known simply as Obexer's and dating from the 1930's, is also farther to the south, its faded-red boat storage buildings bordering on the highway. Among these buildings is one with dormers and a ragged exterior, originally built around 1920 as a "playhouse" for Walter Hobart, Jr., son of the flamboyant 19th century mining magnate and lumber baron, Walter Hobart, Sr.; within this building was then installed an ancient Otis elevator, one of the first few to be manufactured by the Indiana-based company. Also to be seen here, directly across the road from the Obexer buildings, is a

M.S. Dixie on the lake

Winter at Squaw Valley, site of the 1960 Winter Olympic Games

Scenic Lake Tahoe, viewed from Mt. Pluto on the north shore

Skiing at Northstar-at-Tahoe

twin-roofed, barn-like cottage, dating from 1929. Until quite recently, it housed the "Squirrel's Nest," a delightful little shop-cum-restaurant where notables from San Francisco could often be seen on weekend summer afternoons, milling about and rummaging through countless rare and curiously enchanting gifts.

Homewood has a few other outstanding older buildings to be seen alongside of the highway as well, with one or two of them especially interesting in their locally-quarried stone and native timber construction. The splendid Rockwood Lodge, located just to the north of the Obexer buildings, on the opposite side of the highway, is a typical example of this post-Prohibition Era architecture. It features a rock-wall exterior — believed to be the work of the same stonemason who is credited with creating the marvel of the famed "Fleur du Lac" farther north on the west shore — and a lovely knotty pine interior. The lodge was originally built as a summer home in 1936, by one Carlos Rookwood, a prosperous dairyman (and sometime bootlegger) from Vallejo. The lodge is now a charming bed and breakfast establishment, beautifully restored to its former glory.

Also worth visiting at Homewood are a couple of countrified restaurants, including the Grubstake Cafe, a casual diner that has long been a favorite of skiers. Then, too, at the northern end of the Homewood Ski Area is to be found a touch of old Switzerland, the Swiss Lakewood Restaurant, built quite like a European hunting lodge. Opposite the Swiss restaurant is a unique seaplane base, the only one of its kind at the lake, from where seaplane rides can be taken over the lake for some spectacular aerial sightseeing; and during the summer months, noted opera singers and chamber orchestras from San Francisco and elsewhere perform in the outdoor area adjacent to the seaplane base, offering yet an added attraction to the west shore visitor.

Chambers Landing and Tahoma

Leaving Homewood, the highway circles a granite bulge near the southeast corner of McKinney Bay, then turns directly south. About fifty yards or so from the curve, a side road leads off toward the lake, down to historic Chambers Landing, where one can visit a lovely sandy beach and a fabulous 1870's over-water clubhouse perched at the end of an odd-shaped pier, now serving as a cocktail bar and lounge. This is, of course, the oldest such clubhouse at the lake, a glorious reminder of the "Gay 90's" when scores of over-water saloons and clubhouses burst upon the Lake Tahoe shoreline. Expansive, all around views can be enjoyed from here.

Just over a mile down the road from Chambers Landing lies Tahoma (meaning "home away from home"), a more or less self-contained settlement with a post office, a knotty pine store, a saloon, a pizzeria, a family restaurant, two real estate offices, and more than a half dozen lodges. Of interest here is one beautifully restored, pre-World War II building with brown and white trim and spacious dormers, located on the west side of the highway; originally an ice house, this now houses the Alpenhaus, a traditional Swiss country inn and restaurant which, surprisingly, also serves authentic Basque food on certain days of the

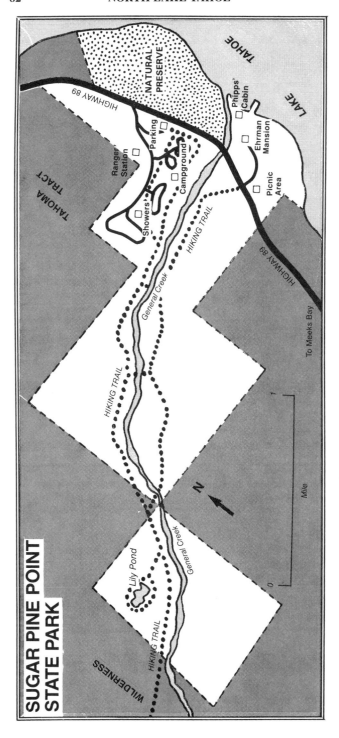

week. Receded farther west from the highway, however, the Tahoma residential tract is much like a city suburb, with numbered streets and right angle intersections, though several old, hut-like cabins are still to be found nestled amid the firs here, characteristic in their antiquated stone chimney constructions. Tahoma is also extremely popular with North Tahoe's "locals," who continue to populate the area in growing numbers, making this one of the largest local communities on the west shore.

Sugar Pine Point State Park

The Sugar Pine Point State Park is one of the loveliest of Lake Tahoe's parklands, bordered on the southwest by the northern portion of the high-country Desolation Wilderness, and on the north by the Tahoma tract. There are nearly 2000 acres of parkland here, abundant in splendid trees and wooded trails, with three or four points of historic interest as well. One of the highlights of the park that no one should miss, is the Ehrman Mansion, a magnificent, gabled and turreted three-story edifice, built in 1903 and billed as "the finest High Sierra summer home in California." The mansion sits on a rise of ground just back from the lake, reached via a small, almost inconspicuous side road, east off the highway. A lovely walk through an open meadow to the north of the mansion will also take you to it. The mansion faces east over the lake, with its front grounds tumbling down to the water's edge along a dramatic, green slope populated with groves of stately pines and gnarled cedars. Upon these grounds the Ehrmans and the Hellmans — two fabulously wealthy families from San Francisco, related by marriage, and owners of the estate — hosted lavish buffet luncheons in the summers during the "Roaring 20's"; here were to be seen white-shirted butlers bearing laden trays, swarming about between tables overflowing with exotic foods and imported wines, and guests of social standing, strolling leisurely upon the rolling green lawns. The grounds now provide for some beautiful, shaded picnic areas, to be enjoyed by the general public. At the bottom of the slope one can view an ancient L-shaped pier and two equally ancient boat-houses. Also on the shoreline here is to be seen the preserved stump of a 4-foot wide juniper tree that was once described by the renowned naturalist John Muir as "the largest and the finest in the Sierra." Surrounding the mansion are a series of smaller structures worth investigating, including a water tower and a power generating plant, servants' quarters, stables and carriage house, and a caretaker's cabin; there is even a tennis court to be found here. The mansion is now an interpretive center of sorts, open to the public during summer. It was acquired by the California State Parks Division in 1965, together with the rest of the estate, for a reported $8,000,000.

North and south of the mansion are two other places of interest: General Phipps' Cabin and the site of the old Bellevue Hotel. The hotel site is just south of the mansion, at the edge of the lake, now overgrown with tall pines and firs. The Bellevue Hotel, a lure of its day, was built on this site in 1888 and gutted by fire in 1893. Particularly well patronized was its white, over-water clubhouse with lattice verandahs; this was also the only building to have survived the fire, and was later shipped across to the southwest corner of the lake, plank by plank, and rebuilt as the Cascade House. The Phipps' cabin, north of the Ehrman home, still stands upon the lakeshore, and in its own tumbledown way it is really quite delightful. The cabin was originally built in the early 1860's by General William Phipps, a famous Indian fighter from Kentucky, who settled here to lead a quiet life of fishing and hunting, homesteading some 160 acres along these shores. Named for the General are the General Creek Campground situated in the park on the west side of the highway, the Phipps' Lake which is farther out west in the Desolation Wilderness, the Phipps' Peak which lies just south of the Rubicon Peak, rising to a height of 9234 feet, and the General Creek that meanders enchantingly through here. There is also a Phipps' Pass in the high country wilderness.

The park, of course, is named for that most majestic of conifers, the Sugar Pine, known to grow to heights of around 200 feet and to live to a ripe old age of anywhere between 300 and 500 years. Its cones mature in approximately two years, often remaining on the tree for another year or so, unless broken off by birds or squirrels earlier; and it is believed that in the early times the Washoe Indians liked to chew on the sweet sugar pine gum derived from these cones, as a sort of candy. Sugar Pines are said to have dominated the forest here until the 1880's, at which time large scale lumbering took its toll, stripping virtually all of Tahoe's forests of their virgin timber. Some fine second-growth Sugar Pines are now to be seen in the park, however, distinguished by their large, flat crowns and branches that join the trunk at right angles. Other growths in the park include Jefferey pines, lodgepoles, red and white firs, incense cedars, black cottonwoods, mountain alders and quaking aspens. In the open meadows, of which there are many in the park, one may find lupine, pussy paw, Indian paintbrush, and a variety of shrubs and wildflowers.

Sugar Pine Point has several enchanting walks to offer too (some of them substituting for nordic ski trails in winter), with stream crossings and wooded picnic areas to be encountered throughout. Notable among these trails is one that explores the "natural preserve" set aside on the east side of the highway. This is the Edward F. Dolder Nature Trail, especially interesting to nature buffs, for it passes through a sanded open meadow where many young, developing plant communities can be observed, which, some day, it is hoped, will evolve into lush forest growths. Another, the Beaudry Trail, passes to the south of the same meadow, with a dozen or so informative, historical markers to be seen alongside of it at intervals. Along this trail one can also view a weather-beaten section of a "Corduroy Road," built in 1882 as part of the great wagon road from Tahoe City to Sugar Pine Point; a "Corduroy Road" was built from logs laid adjacent to one another and held in place by tightly packed soil, usually in places where the earth was too loose to support a gravel road, such as here, where the granite sand has crept into the park. Beyond the "Corduroy" remnants the trail climbs a knoll atop which is to be found the Ehrman Mansion, and just east of here are a handful of small, sandy beaches. There are many other delightful walks to be enjoyed in the western section of the park as well, with one 5½ mile trail following along General Creek, presenting one with some idyllic scenery much of the way; a worthwhile diversion leads to the lovely Lily Pond. The park is also an ideal base from which to explore the northern parts of the more remote Desolation Wilderness, with trails leading to the Lost Lake, and Genevieve, Crag, Shadow, Hidden, Stony Ridge and Cliff lakes.

South to D.L. Bliss State Park

South from the Sugar Pine Point State Park one first arrives at Meeks Bay, a beautifully sheltered cove with a magnificent, mile-long white sand beach. This was the site of Washoe Indian summer camps in centuries past, with fishing and hunting being the principal pursuits. Several arrowheads from those times have been found here on the beach in as recently as the early 1900's. Inland from the bay are to be seen flatlands covered with shrubs, once the scene of much farming, cattle grazing and dairying, and later on, in the 1870's and 1880's, the focus of vast logging operations. Fronting on the highway one sees a knotty pine fire station, where the annual Loggers' Olympics are held each summer, as well as some special picture slide shows once in a while, featuring topics of outdoor interest. Back from the fire station is to be found the Meeks Bay Resort, one of the most popular, flourishing campground resorts of Tahoe, with a store, a gift shop, bike rentals, a pier and some charming little cabins that date from the early 1900's. In fact, many of the structures seen at Meeks Bay date back to the earlier part of this century, including the Meadow Park Store and the cluster of tumbledown buildings nearby. A second campground is to be found nestled along the promontory south of the crescent-shaped bay.

Immediately below Meeks Bay is the equally interesting but much wider Rubicon Bay. The south corner of the bay is described by a large, 600-foot promontory, beneath which the shoreline drops a sheer 1411 feet, vertically; this, incidentally, is the deepest point along the lake's shoreline, known as Rubicon Point. Above the bay can be seen a set of thinly forested hills, dotted with expensive mountain homes. These are the Rubicon Hills, and the lack of large-tree coverage here has really become quite an asset, with most of the homes enjoying unobstructed, panoramic views of the lake and the Sierra. Bearing the name "Rubicon" also, are a creek, a small wilderness lake, a mountain range, and the lakefront tract just below the highway here. And "Rubicon," we are told, is named for an ancient Roman river of the same name, made famous by Caesar's crossing of it. It is said that the backcountry wilderness in these parts was so remote about a century or so ago, that the mountain men attempting to cross it, compared it to Caesar's perilous crossing of the river Rubicon, and so gave it the same name.

Adjoining Rubicon on the south is the D.L. Bliss State Park, a 957-acre preserve with 14,640 feet of shoreline. The park is named for one of Lake Tahoe's great legends, Duane LeRoy Bliss, a lumbering giant who at one time owned more than three-quarters of Tahoe's lakefront land. In fact, this very acreage was Bliss-owned until donated by the family to the State of California in about 1930. It is of interest to note that Bliss also owned the largest fleet of Tahoe's steamers and tug boats, including the legendary *Tahoe*, as well as the narrow-gauge Lake Tahoe Railroad that shuffled down the Truckee River Canyon in the early 1900's, linking Tahoe City to the railroad town of Truckee. Even the fabled Tahoe Tavern and the Glenbrook estate, about which so much has been said and written, was owned by the enormously wealthy Bliss family.

The Bliss park, however, is notable for mainly two things: its lovely, wooded campground, with nearly 200 campsites; and its splendid array of fine rocks. Of the latter it can be said that nowhere at the lake are so many large, well-rounded rocks to be found in one place, as here. Particularly interesting among these is the Balancing Rock, an enormous mass of granite, wonderfully balanced on a natural pedestal, located just inside the park. The rock makes for an excellent subject for camera buffs, especially striking in its size which is several times that of a full-statured human, and its shape, which is supposed to vaguely resemble the head of a certain Indian chief who is said to have been buried here long, long ago. This again is a romanticized version from an enchanting Indian legend which tells of the formation of the rock. According to the legend, there once dwelled upon these shores a tribe of giant Indians. And in the waters off shore lived a wicked, giant serpent. Several tribesmen, while fishing in these waters, had been lost to the serpent's wrath over a period of time, and the tribe lived in great fear of the monster. One day, however, the great chief of the tribe who always sat in the very same spot where the rock is now to be seen, decided to slay the serpent and put an end to the misery of his people. He prepared his long knives and his bow and arrows, and went out in a boat to meet the serpent. He waited until the serpent showed its head above the water, then shot his arrows into its head. But the serpent remained alive. So then the chief lunged at the beast with a drawn knife, and a fierce battle ensued. The entire tribe gathered on the shore to watch their brave chief do battle with the wicked serpent. Many times the chief and the serpent disappeared beneath the water, but then resurfaced, until one final time they went down, not to appear again. Just then a storm broke out, lasting a whole day. When the storm subsided the following day, the bodies of both the chief and the serpent, bloodied and lifeless, washed up on shore. The tribes-people carried the body of their brave chief to his favorite spot where he had sat for so many years, looking out over the lake, and there they buried him, leaving his head above the ground so that he may continue to look out over his beloved "Big Blue." This, then, is the head of the giant chief, and the supporting pedestal his neck.

Also of interest at the Bliss State Park is a short, self-guided trail that leads to the site of an old lighthouse atop the Rubicon Point pro-montory. At the base of the outcropping is a walled-in area that offers picnicking possibilities and great views of the lake. From here you can also get a closer look at the deep blue waters of what is the deepest point on Lake Tahoe's shoreline. The colors in these waters are re-markable, changing from a pale shade of blue to deep indigo, almost blue-black; (in 1889, a *Sacramento Daily Record Union* reporter is known to have joked about using these waters as a bluing solution for Yankee uniforms). Just north of here lie two delightful sandy beaches, and to the south a series of imaginatively named rocks, including Hen and Chickens, Four Loaves of Bread, Turk in Turban, Grinning Negro and Frog Rock. These are mostly seen from the water. A little farther to the south is a shy little recess in the shoreline, known as "Grecian

Bend''; it is named after the walk practised by American women in the 1920's, and is said to resemble their padded rears. Also worth pursuing here is a beautiful 4½-mile walk that starts out by the beaches to the north, tracing the shoreline of the park south, then passes into the adjoining Emerald Bay State Park, leading eventually to the much-talked-about Vikingsholm in the cradle of Emerald Bay. This is an especially picturesque walk, for it follows closely the lakeshore much of the way.

THE NORTH SHORE

The north shore, as the name suggests, rings the northern portion of the lake, from northeast of Tahoe City to Incline Village and Sand Harbor, encompassing nearly 20 miles of shoreline. Here the atmospheric clarity and the overtly generous high altitude sunshine become at once apparent, and are often cited as being the principal lures to the area. The north shore is also noted for its many natural wonders, among them the "Sunken Cliffs" off Dollar's Point, the "Hot Springs" of Brockway, the two-story high boulders off the north Stateline Point, the astonishing transparency of Agate and Crystal Bays, and the dozens of secluded coves just south of Sand Harbor where clusters of rocks emerge above the water to naturally enclose swimming areas. Then, too, there are the man-made wonders: four alpine ski areas — Northstar, Mount Rose, Ski Incline and Slide Mountain — four golf courses, two of them championship, 18-hole courses, a couple of miniature golfing alleys, several picnic and recreation areas, including the fabled Ponderosa Ranch (the set for TV's *Bonanza* series), and even some casinos.

A half dozen or so small detours provide for additional interest in the north shore. The area's main artery, Highway 28, part of which forms the North Lake Boulevard and part the Tahoe Boulevard, actually has two other highways branching from it — 267 (North Shore Boulevard) and 27 (Mount Rose Highway). 267 passes over the 7199-foot Brockway Summit to Truckee, with the Northstar Resort being reached at an approximate halfway point. The Mount Rose Highway winds through several miles of pine country to escape over the eastern Sierra range into Nevada's desert valleys; the low-lying, barren hills farther east from the valleys lie in deep contrast to the High Sierra. Other detours lead to Marlette Lake, the Spooner Lake State Park, and along Incline's shoreline by way of the famous "Lakeshore Drive," each inviting special attention.

The Northwest

Leaving Tahoe City on North Lake Boulevard (Highway 28), one first arrives at Lake Forest, a wooded tract set slightly back from the highway. Lake Forest is an old settlement, dating back to 1859 when a real floating island, Island Farm, operated as a guest ranch just off the shores from here. The area was then also famous for giant vegetables grown on its soil, among which was one memorable, record-sized turnip measuring 16½ inches in diameter. Foremost among Lake Forest's attractions today is the Fish and Game Department's Hatchery, located at the corner of the highway and Lake Forest Road, and housed in a charming, turn-of-the-century gnarled cedar building; it can be toured with prior arrangement with the department. South from the hatchery, down to the lake, extends the open meadow of the Lake Forest Campground, a favorite with summer vacationers. A small beach fringes on the green square, and nearby are located the U.S. Coast Guard Station and a public boat-launching ramp. Within Lake Forest, nestled along Lake Forest Road which loops through the subdivision in a semi-circle to re-emerge on the highway one-half mile along, are to be found several shops, a lumber yard, a few motels, and Bacchi's, an Italian inn and restaurant that has been passed down the family from generation to generation for the last some 60 years, considered to be one of the finest homegrown Italian restaurants in the neighborhood.

One-quarter mile above Lake Forest sits Dollar Hill, named for Robert Stanley Dollar, Sr., a San Francisco shipping magnate who owned much of the tract from 1927 until its subdivision only a few decades ago. The "hill" drops off sharply to the northeast and southwest along the highway, and to the southeast along a peninsular tract that converges into a point, variously known as Chinquapin, Old Lousy, Observatory and Dollar's Point. Here, it is told, that one George Flick proposed to build an observatory at a cost of $1,000,000 in 1873, but ended up placing it on Mount Hamilton above Santa Clara. Off Dollar's Point, however, are to be found some of the most treasured underwater marvels of Lake Tahoe, often clearly visible on fine, calm days. A slow boat ride along here, from just south of the Point to just past it, reveals what have come to be known as the "Sunken Cliffs." Here the lake floor drops from a depth of around 30 feet to a sheer 600 feet within some 50 yards or so, creating illusions of falling off a cliff; this, in fact, is what Mark Twain was referring to when he wrote about his fantastic "balloon voyages" on the lake. Two such "cliffs" run almost parallel to one another, like miniature canyons, some one-half mile apart. Beyond the "cliffs" can be discerned broad steps descending into the deep blue, known as the "Tahoe Flats" — an excellent area for trolling for Mackinaw trout in spring and early summer.

North of Dollar Point the highway curves around a twin cove to a protruding land mass known as Flick Point, which takes its name from the Flick Brothers who fished here, commercially, for several years. Interestingly, the Flick Brothers, William, John and Nicholas, was each born on Christmas Day of 1841, 1847 and 1850, respectively, with William passing away in April of 1929, John on April 9, 1938, and Nicholas on April 19, 1938; a coincidental fact worthy of record books. The bay sheltered in these waters is the Carnelian Bay, named for the reddish-brown semi-precious stones found in abundance on its sandy beach by a survey party in 1860. The tract of the same name lies just south of Flick Point, boasting a post office, fire station, lumber yard, several shops, a miniature golf course, and a distinctively large, bright-blue boat storage and marina known as the Sierra Boat Company, where some lovely antique boats can be viewed. The old post office is now a snug little coffee shop, located on the north side of the highway, and for jazz buffs there is the Carnelian House, a restaurant of sorts situated on the lake, where live jazz music can be heard on weekends. Carnelian Bay is also the scene of one of the most endearing tales of Lake Tahoe: "the hole in the bottom of the lake." It was about a mile off the Carnelian shores, as the tale goes, that a whirlpool was discovered in 1869 by one William Meeker, a vacationing stock speculator from San Francisco. Meeker quickly learned that the whirlpool had its origins in a hole in the bottom of the lake, one that tunneled beneath the lake floor to emerge in a Virginia City silver mine, the Savage Mine, many miles to the east. This startling discovery Meeker shared with one Colonel Clair, an unscrupulous stock trader, also from San Francisco. And the colonel had an idea . . . The two men carved out a conical-shaped "plug" from a 5-foot log to plug the hole with. Armed with this they were able to flood the shaft of the Savage Mine, or dry it out, practically at will, and thereby manipulate the company's stock: when the plug was out of the hole, the mine would remain flooded, the stock would plummet and the colonel and Meeker would buy; when the plug was in the hole, the mine would dry out, the stock would sky-rocket and they would sell out. Thus, within a week the colonel and Meeker cleaned up a cool couple of million dollars through manipulation of the Savage Mining Company's stock. Then one night the colonel cleaned out Meeker, knocked him unconscious, lowered his body into the hole in the bottom of the lake, and plugged the hole with the hand-crafted stopper. The body, of course, washed up in the sump of the Savage Mine several days later, mysteriously, needless to say; but the plug has remained in place ever since, its location a well-guarded secret of Colonel Clair's. Curiously, there is a Colonel Clair's restaurant located on the highway just north of Carnelian Bay, housed in a stately cedar building with a green shingled roof.

Inland from Carnelian Bay, high on a rise of ground, is to be found the Agate Bay subdivision where in the 1920's the Agate Bay Hotel was located, said to have been patronized by such luminaries as Theodore Roosevelt and Jack Dempsey. The hotel burned down in the 1940's.

About a mile farther, just north of Flick Point, one encounters what has been dubbed "the motel capital of North Lake Tahoe," Tahoe Vista. Motels flank the highway in virtually unbroken rows, several of them edging south to the lake. Many of these were built only some three decades ago, for the anticipated Squaw Valley Winter Olympic Games of 1960. Some excellent restaurants are to be found wedged between the motels along the highway, among them Chez Lylianne, a charming French restaurant, and La Playa, formerly Bon Vivant, where French seafood is served in an intimate setting with framed windows overlooking the lake. La Playa is actually housed in the old, native stone Kellogg Mansion, once the summer home of the legendary cereal king; it was built around 1910. Two marinas, too, are to be found at Tahoe Vista, the Tahoe Vista Marina and Alpine Marina. The Tahoe Vista Marina is especially interesting with its long, L-shaped pier, which was built in the early 1900's to enable the 169-foot steamer *Tahoe* to dock in these waters while making its scheduled "mail stops."

Propped at the marina is another delightful French-seafood restaurant, Captain Jon's, and beside it the greatly talked about Le Petit Pier. A couple of fine sandy beaches grace the Tahoe Vista shoreline, popular with summer crowds. Receded back from the shoreline is a preserved square mile of green, the North Tahoe Regional Park, and to the east of it the 9-hole Woodvista Golf Course, previously known as the Brockway Golf Course.

Northstar

6 miles north of the Tahoe Vista – Kings Beach area, just off Highway 267, lies Northstar (at-Tahoe), a 2500-acre, self-contained resort complex with clusters of condominiums, on-site lodging for tourists, alpine and nordic ski areas, a couple of restaurants, a general store, horse stables, and even an 18-hole golf course. Northstar is one of the north shore's newest resorts, built mostly in the early 1970's. It is also one of the world's first computer-designed recreation areas where such considerations as drainage, erosion, foliage, snowfall accumulations and grades were computer-analyzed to determine the best locations for the ski slopes, the condominium developments, paved streets, golf course and other recreational facilities. Through much of the 1970's the federal Environmental Protection Agency used Northstar as a demonstration project to illustrate the conservation of environment in modern development, and in 1971 the highly respected Sierra Club described it as a "model development."

Northstar has also been described as an "intermediate skier's paradise." In fact, it currently ranks among Lake Tahoe's "Big Five" ski areas (the other four being Squaw Valley, Alpine Meadows, Heavenly Valley and Kirkwood). Of interest, too, is Northstar's Recreation Center where an Olympic swimming pool, a 25-foot jacuzzi and a dozen or so tennis courts are to be found. During summer an arts and crafts market flourishes at the Northstar village, and in spring, hiking and horseback trails can be enjoyed through the abounding fir-clad mountain country and broad meadows covered with snowplant stalks and freshly-blossomed native wildflowers. Fishing is usually good in the adjoining Martis Creek, a tributary of Martis Lake. To be also recommended is the Schaffer's Mill restaurant, a distinguished steakhouse and seafood establishment where live music is featured on many evenings; the restaurant takes its name, quite appropriately, from Schaffer's Camp, a logging camp that flourished in these parts in the 1870's, supplying lumber for the Virginia City mines.

Kings Beach, Brockway and Crystal Bay

Back on Highway 28 (North Lake Boulevard), one enters the Kings Beach area to the west of the intersection of Highways 28 and 267. Kings Beach is seemingly one of the most commercialized sections of North Lake Tahoe, where much haphazard development has occurred in previous years. The highway through here widens into four lanes, with a profusion of shops, restaurants, fast-food places and motels crowding along the sides. One of the chief attractions here is the beach

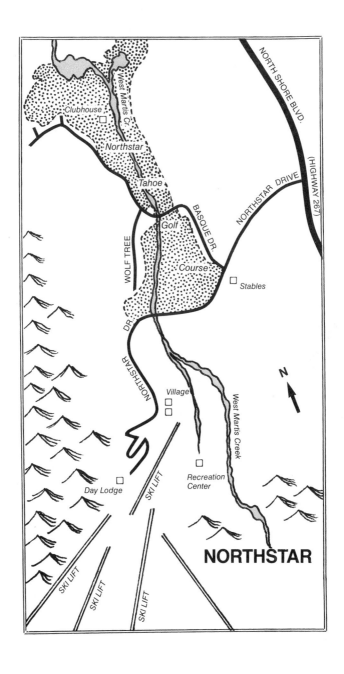

NORTHSTAR

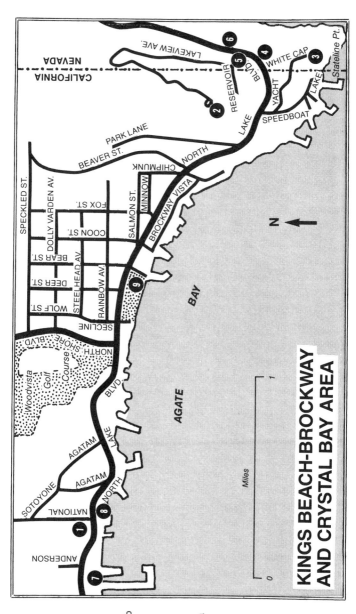

KINGS BEACH-BROCKWAY AND CRYSTAL BAY AREA

Points of Interest
1) Library
2) Stateline Fire Lookout
3) Cal-Neva Club
4) Crystal Bay Club
5) Tahoe Biltmore
6) Kelly's Nugget
7) Tahoe Vista Marina
8) The Boathouse
9) Placer County Recreation Area

area, known as the Placer County Recreation Area, where lies one of the longest and most beautiful sandy beaches of the north shore. In the summer months the beach is inundated with sun-seekers, wind-surfers, joggers, walkers, bikini-clad maidens, suntanned Greek gods, and scores of vacationers sprawled beneath brightly-colored beach umbrellas.

Indeed, Kings Beach is a summer community that flowers in sunny weather. Many of the stores spill over onto the sidewalks in summer, displaying a myriad of "Tahoe" souvenirs and sporting goods, and eateries, too, move out of doors, sporting striped canopies and freshly-painted patio chairs and tables. In the open space adjacent to the highway intersection of highways 28 and 267 the Pro Arts Festival blossoms each July and August, featuring several canvas-covered stalls where local artists and craftsmen display a bounty of hand-crafted merchandise, including pottery, leather goods, stained glass, semi-precious jewelry, wood carvings, imitation Navajo rugs, torch-molded copper decorations, some admirable sculpture, and even oil paintings and water colors inspired by the surrounding scenery. Actually, Kings Beach, while outwardly somewhat shabby, is a mecca of artists, musicians and other culturally oriented folk, though many of them struggling. There are two modest art galleries of interest here, and worth visiting too is a unique French restaurant, La Chiminee, expensive but inspiring.

At the eastern end of Kings Beach rises the Brockway Hill, ascending sharply to the north Stateline where gambling casinos border on the Nevada side. Brockway is really the western tract of the Stateline, dropping off south to the Stateline Point. And here on the south side of the highway, west of the large promontory jutting out at the Stateline, are to be found the famous Brockway Hot Springs, supposedly endowed with medicinal qualities and bubbling forth at a sizzling 147°F. From the late 1800's and until the mid 1900's the Brockway Hot Springs Hotel stood at the site of the springs, luring health-seekers and vacationers alike, and prompting the building of the Hot Springs-Martis Valley Road (Highway 267) earlier in 1869. But in 1970 the hotel gave way to the present day luxury condominium development, the Brockway Springs Resort, where the hot mineral water is now piped into every apartment, available at the turn of a faucet. Vacation rentals are available at the resort, however.

Brockway is also noted for its shoreline (the Brockway-Stateline shoreline), where several fascinating rock formations can be observed; these date back thousands of years to the ice age when a gigantic glacier filled the lake's trough, pushing huge masses of rocks and boulders ahead of it as it moved northeast. Some of the submerged boulders, easily visible through the crystal clear waters, are extraordinary in size, a few of them as large as two-story houses.

The Nevada side of the Stateline is known as Crystal Bay, named for the bay onto which it fronts. Here at Crystal Bay stand three small, rustic casinos — Crystal Bay Club, Tahoe Biltmore and Jim Kelly's Nugget — with 99¢ breakfasts a common feature. Although not quite of the stature of South Lake Tahoe's fastidious, multi-storied hotel-casinos, these north shore clubs nevertheless provide a wide range of gambling opportunities and even some live entertainment. Another Crystal Bay club, the Cal-Neva, straddles the stateline to the south of here, nearer Stateline Point; the stateline actually runs through the club and can be seen painted on the face of the rock wall in its lobby. Notable, too, is the club's gabled magnificence; especially interesting is its brown shingled roof, enormous and acutely pitched, with tiny, framed dormers peeking out from above. On either side of the club, some splendid, twisted roads wind quietly down to the Stateline Point, with clusters of dark-gray rocks randomly strewn alongside; a couple of interesting residences can be seen majestically perched above the rocks, looking out over the vast, shaded blue of the lake.

Northwest of the Crystal Bay casinos is to be found the Stateline Fire Lookout, a rare vantage point for those picturesque, sweeping views of Lake Tahoe. Reservoir Lane which flanks the Tahoe Biltmore parking lot on the east, Lakeview Avenue, and a Forest Service road that branches off Lakeview and loops back into the California side of the Stateline, lead to the Lookout.

Incline Village

Incline Village lies at the head of Crystal Bay (the actual bay), some two miles from Stateline. This is the most notable and prosperous of the north shore communities, where the 'trickle down' affluence has reached virtually every corner of the "village." Here the residents own their ski area, Ski Incline, as well as two golf courses and a couple of beautiful beaches. The sense of well being, however, is perhaps never more apparent than on the famous Lakeshore Drive, the avenue of the affluent and the wealthy; palatial homes, the likes of which aren't to be readily found anywhere else at the lake, at least not in such clusters, stand in unabashed oppulence on the lake side of the road. Here, too, is the north shore's most prestigious hotel, the Hyatt, at the corner of Country Club Drive. The high property values of Incline's real estate and the corresponding property taxes have no doubt become a lively source of income for the county in which the village is situated, namely Washoe County, the seat of which lies in Reno; this has led several Renoites to nickname the neighborhood "income village," with fondness no doubt.

In actual fact, though, Incline derives its name from the "Incline Mountain" located just northeast of the business district, upon which an early day engineering marvel manifested itself. Here on Incline Mountain was built a tramway in 1874, straight up the side of the mountain, some 4000 feet in length, with a vertical rise of 1400 feet and a gradient of approximately 67%. Two tracks ran parallel to one another to the summit, and angled flat cars, specially designed for the task, carried full loads of logs to the very top, discharging them into a V-shaped log-chute which in turn passed through a 4000-foot water tunnel down the other side of the mountain, from where the logs were then railroaded across to the Virginia City mines. Two giant bullwheels were used in the operation, each 12 feet in diameter, with wire cables fed around them and hitched to the tops of the cars (a total of more than 8000 feet of cable was used). The summit wheel was driven by a 40-horsepower steam engine anchored in granite blocks, and the upward haul of each laden car was aided greatly by the counterweight of the downward bound car — a principle so commonly employed in cable car operations. This, then, was "The Great Incline Tramway," an early day sight pointed out by cruise-boat captains to their vacationing passengers as they rounded Crystal Bay. The tramway was dismantled in 1897 after nearly 200,000,000 board feet of lumber and more than a million cords of wood had been transported by way of it.

The lure of Incline today is its vacation ambiance, with facilities to complement. There are four alpine ski areas in the mountains surrounding the village: Ski Incline, Mount Rose, Slide Mountain and Northstar. There are two golf courses here, the 18-hole Incline Championship Course measuring 7120 yards, and the Incline Executive Green, a 9-hole course. There are two major shopping centers: the Christmas Tree Village with its collection of novelty stores and ethnic restaurants, and the Raley's Center which is the larger of the two, with two chain stores, a large sporting goods store, a bookshop, several clothing and gift stores, and a couple of real estate offices. Then also there are two tennis clubs, a Chamber of Commerce and several smaller shopping malls, such as by the Hyatt and at Mays Boulevard. Dozens of other stores front on the highway, which here is known as Tahoe Boulevard, and a marina at the west end of town offers boating enthusiasts opportunities. Vacation rentals and real estate sales are keenly pursued in the village.

Incline also enjoys a relatively large spread, nearly nine square miles in area, with some leisurely drives to be taken through it, quite at random really. The tree-lined Country Club Drive, for one, enchantingly passes by both golf courses, the soft green pastels making for some delightful viewing; Fairway Boulevard, Driver Way and Golfers Pass Road actually cut through the manicured greens for a more intimate drive yet. Ski Way is another worthwhile drive, with many miles of mountain country to enjoy enroute to the ski slopes; along here is also to be found the Potlatch, an exotic gallery-store where designer stuffed animals and Swiss music boxes can be appreciated, and the Tyrolian Village where cheerful, European chalets stand in a cluster. Farther out from the village the Mount Rose Highway climbs to more than 1000 feet above lake level, winding through lush, pine-clad terrain, then descends into the sculpted, barren valleys east of the Sierra, providing the motorist with a bewildering contrast that brings out the mystique in mountain country. Along the Mount Rose Highway one can also enjoy a panoramic viewpoint at an elevation of 7595 feet, from where one of the most fabulous views of Lake Tahoe can be captured on camera.

Ponderosa Ranch

Another attraction at Incline Village, nestled along its southeast corner and to be highly recommended for family entertainment, is the Ponderosa Ranch, a lovely western theme park with an Old West town, horse stables, western museums, and acres upon acres of ranchland rolling back into the mountains to the east. The ranch, however, is

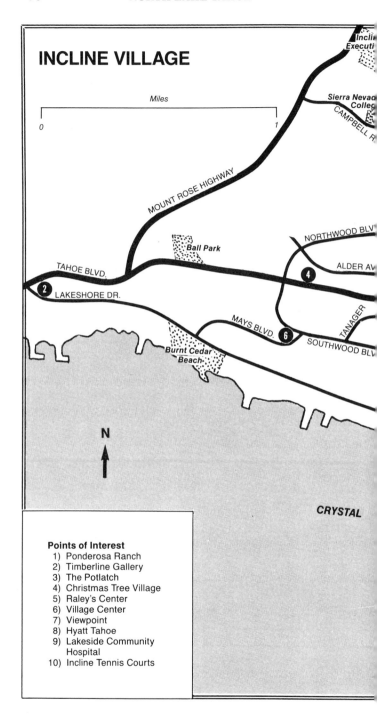

INCLINE VILLAGE

Miles

0   1

Incli
Executi

Sierra Neva
Colleg

CAMPBELL R

MOUNT ROSE HIGHWAY

Ball Park

NORTHWOOD BLV

TAHOE BLVD.

ALDER AV

④

② LAKESHORE DR.

MAYS BLVD.

TANAGER

⑥

SOUTHWOOD BLV

Burnt Cedar
Beach

N

CRYSTAL

Points of Interest
1) Ponderosa Ranch
2) Timberline Gallery
3) The Potlatch
4) Christmas Tree Village
5) Raley's Center
6) Village Center
7) Viewpoint
8) Hyatt Tahoe
9) Lakeside Community
     Hospital
10) Incline Tennis Courts

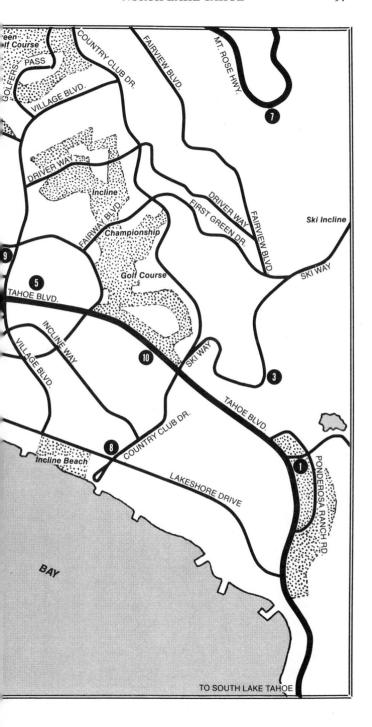

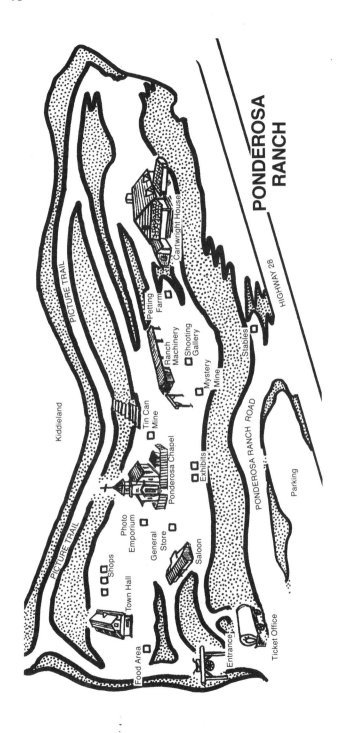

PONDEROSA RANCH

HIGHWAY 28

Cartwright House

Petting Farm

Ranch Machinery

Shooting Gallery

Stables

Mystery Mine

PICTURE TRAIL

Tin Can Mine

Kiddieland

Ponderosa Chapel

Exhibits

PONDEROSA RANCH ROAD

Parking

Photo Emporium

General Store

Saloon

PICTURE TRAIL

Shops

Town Hall

Food Area

Entrance

Ticket Office

also the site of the well-known TV series, *Bonanza,* starring Lorne
Green and Michael Landon. In fact, much of what you see here was
built expressly for the series by NBC in 1959. Just above town, at the
southern end, you can visit the legendary Cartwright House, the rambling log home of the Cartwright family where numerous indoor
scenes were filmed on location. Within the house are to be found
several beautifully preserved pieces of antique furniture, each with a
history of its own, and some memorable props from the series, such
as the lovely hand-crafted dining table where the Cartwrights seemed
always to come together, and the carved coat-rack upon which hang
the vests and hats actually worn by the Cartwrights in the series.
Striking also is the outsized, stone fireplace in the living room, where
Ben Cartwright (Lorne Green) posed often before the cameras. Some
of the camera locations, too, can be seen in the ceiling and walls, from
where those marvellous vertical and right angle shots were taken.

And so to the Old West town where the "wild west" atmosphere
has been so wonderfully recreated, with boardwalks, a couple of
1860's saloons, a sheriff's office, a barber's shop, a taxidermist, an
assay office, a "tin can" mine with a weathered, wooden tailing wheel,
and a charming, 19th century chapel which can usually be booked for
weddings. There is also a games arcade located in town, complete
with a shooting gallery, and an old-fashioned ice-cream parlor, as well
as a souvenir store. A few museums boast lavish displays of ancient
firearms and carriages and coaches of sorts, while the town's gravel
road is strewn with an assortment of early-day ranch equipment, cen-
tury-old firepumpers, covered wagons, U.S. Cavalry wagons, and
literally a wealth of other antique objects. One of the highlights of the
tour through the town is the Mystery Mine, or "anti-gravity house,"
where a darkened shaft-like area has been constructed such, with angled floor-boards, ceiling and walls, so as to create a sense of imbal-
ance, and even dizziness; here one must stand at an approximate 45-
degree angle to the floor to attain balance, for it is virtually impossible
to stand dead straight without falling over. Often you can hear the
high-pitched laughter enamating from within; this is, of course, from
people undergoing that unique, one-of-a-kind experience of trying to
stand upright, with little success.

The ranch also features an outdoor eatery at the northern end of
the western town, where juicy "Hossburgers" are a favorite. Directly
across from the eatery is a petting farm, especially popular with children; at the farm can be seen a variety of animals, including a mountain
goat and a real, live bison. Another worthwhile pursuit at the
Ponderosa is a guided horseback trail ride through the delightful back-
country, which is all the more rewarding as it offers some spectacular
views of the lake and the Sierra from several points enroute.

Sand Harbor and South

Two and one-half miles south of the Ponderosa Ranch lies Sand
Harbor, North Lake Tahoe's favorite summer recreation area, where
several open-air music festivals and theater performances are held each
July and August; *Romeo and Juliet, As You Like It, Taming of the
Shrew,* and other Shakespeare plays are enacted by members of well-

known theater groups from San Francisco and elsewhere. In the late 1800's, Sand Harbor was the scene of dozens of lavish parties hosted by Walter Hobart, Sr., a mining magnate who made his first million in the Comstock at the age of 21; Hobart was also associated with Tahoe's lumbering activity, and he even owned the famous "Incline Tramway."

Sand Harbor has some lovely picnic areas and a couple of sweeping sandy crescents to enjoy, with tiny piles of rocks to be seen near the mouths of the crescents, enclosing quiet little pools of water in which to splash around. North and south of the beach areas are nestled a handful of rock-lined, sheltered coves, among them the much-talked-about Hidden Beach, lying about a mile to the north of the harbor and reached via a foot trail from the highway; on-shore fishing is excellent along these rocky banks. Also, from Sand Harbor three or four delightful hiking trails wander off into the Lake Tahoe State Park, which lies just to the east. One of these trails leads to two small but enchanting lakes, the Twin Lakes, passing by some idyllic scenery; another follows along Tunnel Creek in the northeast to arrive at the site of the long-forgotten Tunnel Creek Station, where one can view the ruins of old log-flumes dating from the 1880's.

South along Highway 28 are several more secluded coves and shaded areas, some with small beaches which are mostly frequented by nudists; best known among these is Chimney Bay, nearly three miles south of Sand Harbor. Also along the shoreline (almost directly opposite the Marlette Reservoir), hidden from view and closed to the public, is the legendary "Thunderbird Lodge," now known as Whittel's Castle. It was built in 1939 at an estimated cost of $300,000 by Captain George Whittel, a multi-millionaire from San Francisco. Whittel, at one time, is believed to have owned as much as 14,623 acres in these parts, of which at least 452 acres bordered on the lake, taking in 11 miles of shoreline. Of course, much of this land is now either state-owned or under the jurisdiction of the National Forest Service, making this one of the longest, uninterrupted "green belts" at the lake.

Southeast from Whittel's Castle and the Marlette Reservoir, and receded back a mile or so from the highway, lies Marlette Lake, one of the highest lakes in the region at an elevation of 7700 feet. Marlette Lake in the early days was the lifeblood of the Virginia City mines, supplying the entire mining town with its water needs; in 1887, a record 6,600,000 gallons of water was drained from the lake daily. A rather scenic hiking trail now journeys along the west shore of Marlette Lake.

Also worth visiting here is the Spooner Lake State Park, which, too, is arrived at by way of a detour from Highway 28, eastward. South from Spooner Lake, a great deal of momentuous scenery presents itself, especially astounding where, after the highway leaves the Spooner Junction (intersection of Highways 28 and 50), the lake bursts into view again.

PRACTICAL INFORMATION FOR NORTH LAKE TAHOE

HOW TO GET THERE. By Air. The Reno International Airport, the nearest commercial airport to North Tahoe, is only some 40 miles away. More than a dozen airlines service this airport, including *Air Cal* (800) 424-7225, *American* (800) 433-7300, *Continental* (800) 525-0280, *Delta* (800) 221-1212, *Eastern* (800) 323-7323; *Frontier* (800) 255-5050, *PSA* (800) 854-2902, *Republic* (800) 441-1414, *Sky West* (800) 453-9417, *Sun World* (800) 722-4111, *United* (800) 241-6522, *Western* (800) 227-6105, and *Wien Airlines* (800) 562-5222.

Shuttle-bus services between the Reno airport and North Lake Tahoe are conducted by the *Reno Tahoe Tour Company* (800) 821-1555/(702) 322-2828, and *See Tahoe Tours* (702) 832-0713.

By Bus. Greyhound (702) 323-4511 operates to and from its Truckee depot, linking most major cities to the area.

By Rail. The *Amtrak* rail system services the Truckee terminal, which is situated on Commercial Row. Eastbound services originate in San Francisco, and westbound in Chicago. For information, call (800) 252-2231 in California, or (800) 648-3850 from out of state.

By Car. The main artery into the area is Interstate 80, from the west as well as the east. I-80 passes through Truckee, 15 miles north of the north shore, and Highways 89 and 267 link it to the Tahoe basin. Other routes into North Lake Tahoe are by way of Highways 28, 27, or 89 south.

ACCOMMODATIONS. North Lake Tahoe offers a wide variety in accommodations, including hotels, motels, and vacation rental condominiums and cabins. Reservations, year-round, can be made through the Tahoe North Visitors and Convention Bureau; call toll free (800) 822-5959 in California, or (800) 824-8557 from out of state. Locally, call the Bureau on (916) 583-3494.

Most of the area's hotels and motels accept major credit cards; however, it is advisable to inquire with the respective establishment. Rates, based on double occupancy, are categorized as follows: *Expensive,* over $40; *Moderate,* $29-$40; *Inexpensive,* under $29. (Note: all rates are subject to change, and are generally 15%-25% higher in summer and on weekends and holidays.)

Truckee

Mountain View Inn. *Expensive.* 10154 High St., Truckee. 6 rooms; bed and breakfast. (587-5388)

Hilltop Lodge. *Moderate.* Hwy. 267, Truckee. 21 rooms, TV, phones, spa. (587-2545)

Super 8 Lodge. *Moderate.* Deerfield Drive, West Truckee. 41 rooms, TV, phones, sauna, spa. (587-8888)

Truckee Tahoe Inn. *Moderate.* Hwy. 267, 1 m. S of Truckee. 100 rooms, phones, sauna, jacuzzi, continental breakfast. (587-4525)

Tahoe City and West Shore

Alpenhaus. *Expensive*. 6941 West Lake Blvd., Tahoma. Swiss Country inn; 6 units. Restaurant. (525-5000)

Alpine Motor Inn. *Moderate*. Located in Alpine Meadows. 25 rooms, TV, phones. (583-4266)

Christy Hill Restaurant and Inn. *Expensive*. On Squaw Valley Road in Squaw Valley. 7 units, TV, restaurant. (583-8551)

Cottage Inn. *Expensive*. 1690 West Lake Blvd., Tahoe City. Bed and breakfast inn with individual cottages. Spa. (581-4073)

Fantasy Inn III. *Expensive*. 790 North Lake Blvd., Tahoe City. 33 rooms, TV, phones, in-room spas. (583-8578)

Lake of the Sky Motor Inn. *Moderate*. 955 North Lake Blvd. 22 rooms, TV, phones, pool. (583-3305)

Lakeside House. *Expensive*. 1745 Sequoia Ave., Tahoe City. 5 rooms; bed and breakfast. (583-8796)

Mayfield House. *Expensive*. 236 Grove Street. Stone cottage. Established Old Tahoe bed and breakfast inn. (583-1001)

Pepper Tree Inn. *Expensive*. 645 North Lake Blvd. 51 rooms, TV, phones, pool, and hot tubs. (583-3711)

River Ranch. *Expensive*. Alpine Meadows Road and Highway 89. Old lodge with 22 rooms; TV, phones, and restaurant. (583-4264)

Rockwood Lodge. *Expensive*. 5295 West Lake Blvd., Homewood. Refurbished 1930s lodge with 5 guest rooms; bed and breakfast. (525-4663)

Tahoe City Travelodge. *Expensive*. 455 North Lake Blvd. 47 rooms, TV, phones, pool, hot tubs and restaurant. (583-3766)

Tamarack Lodge Motel. *Inexpensive*. 2311 North Lake Blvd. 19 rooms, TV. (583-3350)

Edwards Tahoe Lodge. *Moderate*. 6845 West Lake Blvd., Tahoma. 17 units, pool. (525-7207)

Homewood Marina Lodge. *Inexpensive*. 5190 West Lake Blvd., Homewood. 17 units. (525-6728)

Homeside Motel & Lodge. *Moderate*. West Lake Blvd., Homewood. 17 rooms, TV, sauna. (525-9990)

North Shore

Blue Vue Lodge. *Moderate*. 8755 North Lake Blvd., Kings Beach. 10 units, TV, pool. (546-3871)

Cedar Glen Lodge. *Moderate*. 6589 North Lake Blvd., Tahoe Vista. 32 units, TV, phones, pool, sauna, spas. (546-4281)

Charmey Chalet Motel. *Expensive*. 6549 North Lake Blvd., Kings Beach. 25 rooms, TV, pool, hot tubs. (546-3301)

Cottonwood Lodge. *Expensive*. Tahoe Vista. 18 units, TV, pool, sauna and spas. (546-2220)

Crown Motel. *Moderate*. 8200 North Lake Blvd., Kings Beach. 39 rooms, TV, phones, pool, spa. (546-3388)

Falcon Motor Lodge. *Moderate*. Highway 28, Kings Beach. 30 units, TV, pool. (546-2236)

Foothill Motel. *Inexpensive*. 8931 North Lake Blvd., Kings Beach. 6 units, TV. (546-3036)

Firelite Lodge. *Moderate*. 7035 North Lake Blvd., Tahoe Vista. 24 units, TV, phones, pool. (546-7222)

Franciscan Lakeside Lodge. *Expensive*. 6944 North Lake Blvd., Tahoe Vista. 58 units, TV, pool. (546-7234)

Goldcrest Resort Motel. *Moderate*. 8194 North Lake Blvd., Kings Beach. 25 rooms, TV, pool, hot tubs. (546-3301)

Horseshoe Lodge. *Moderate*. 6731 North Lake Blvd., Tahoe Vista. 31 units, TV, pool, sauna, spas, and restaurant. (546-3386)

Garni Motor Lodge. *Expensive*. 9937 Highway 28, Kings Beach. 95 rooms, TV, phones, pool, sauna. (546-3341)

Mourelatos' Lakeshore Resort. *Expensive*. 6834 North Lake Blvd., Tahoe Vista. 32 rooms, TV, restaurant. (583-5334)

North Lake Lodge. *Moderate*. 8716 North Lake Blvd., Kings Beach. 20 units, TV, hot tubs. (546-2731)

Rustic Cottage Resort. *Moderate*. 7449 North Lake Blvd., Tahoe Vista. 18 units, TV. (546-3523)

Seven Pines Motel. *Inexpensive*. 279 Bear, Kings Beach. 12 units, TV. (546-9886)

Silver Sands Resort. *Expensive*. Tahoe Vista. 66 rooms, TV, phones, pool, hot tubs. (546-2592)

Stevenson's Holiday Inn. *Moderate*. 8742 North Lake Blvd., Kings Beach. 24 units, TV, phones, pool, sauna, hot tubs. (546-3326)

Tahoya Shore Lodge. *Expensive*. 7610 North Lake Blvd., Tahoe Vista. 28 units, TV, phones, pool. (546-2571)

Thornley Lodge. *Moderate*. 7630 North Lake Blvd., Tahoe Vista. 23 units, TV, pool, spas. (546-3952)

Villa Vista Resort. *Expensive*. 6750 North Lake Blvd., Tahoe Vista. 13 units, TV, phones, pool. (546-3518)

Vista Shores. *Moderate*. 6731 North Lake Blvd., Tahoe Vista. TV, pool, sauna, beach, restaurant. (546-3386)

Incline Village

All Seasons Resort. *Expensive*. 98 units, TV, phones, pool, jacuzzi, sauna. (831-2311)

Haus Bavaria. *Expensive*. P.O. Box 3308, Incline Village, NV 89450. 5 rooms with private baths; bed and breakfast. (831-6122)

Lakeside Tennis & Ski Resort. *Expensive*. 987 Tahoe Blvd., Incline Village. 36 units, TV, phones, pool, jacuzzi. (831-5258)

TELEPHONE AND EMERGENCY. Telephone area codes in North Lake Tahoe are 916 for the California side and 702 for the Nevada side. For emergencies, involving fire, police or ambulance, dial 911.

Specific emergency services include — *Tahoe City Sheriff* (916) 583-4244; *Incline Village Sheriff* (702) 831-0222; *Truckee Sheriff* (916) 587-4611; *El Dorado Sheriff* (916) 544-3464; *Poison Center* (800) 852-7221.

Other important service numbers: *Tahoe Forest Hospital*, Truckee (916) 587-6011; *Lakeside Community Hospital*, Incline Village (702) 831-5755; *California Highway Patrol* (916) 587-3510; *Coast Guard* (916) 583-4433; *Road Conditions*, California (916) 587-3806; *Road Conditions*, Nevada (702) 793-1313.

TOURIST INFORMATION. *Greater North Lake Tahoe Chamber of Commerce*, at the Lighthouse Center in Tahoe City (916) 583-2371; *Incline Village Chamber of Commerce*, at 999 Tahoe Boulevard in Incline Village (702) 831-4440. *Truckee-Donner Chamber of Commerce*, Commercial Row, Truckee (916) 587-2757.

The useful publication, *North Tahoe Week* (freely available outside most area stores), provides information on current tourist activities. Also worthwhile is the bimonthly *Key* magazine, available at the Chambers of Commerce, which contains show information and shopping tips mostly.

HOW TO GET AROUND. By Bus. *TART* (Tahoe Area Regional Transit) operates regular, scheduled services between Meeks Bay/Tahoma and Tahoe City, between Tahoe City and the north Stateline, and between the Stateline and Incline Village. *TART* buses arrive and depart both Meeks Bay and the Stateline on the hour, and service Tahoe City and Incline Village on the half-hour. There are several marked bus stops on West Lake Boulevard (Highway 89) and North Lake Boulevard (Highway 28). Fare is 75¢ one way. For timetables and information, call (916) 581-6365 in California, or (800) 325-TART in Nevada.

In winter, free ski shuttle buses are an integral part of North Tahoe's transport, offering a valued service to some of the ski areas — including Alpine Meadows (916) 583-4232, Squaw Valley (916) 583-6985, Northstar (916) 562-1010, Mount Rose (702) 849-0704, and Ski Incline (702) 832-1177. Call the respective area for information on shuttles.

By Taxi. Four small taxi companies service the North Tahoe area: *Tahoe Cab* (916) 546-3324/(702) 831-1922; *North Shore Taxi* (916) 546-3181; *Incline Taxi* (916) 546-3181; and *Truckee Yellow Cab* (916) 587-6336.

By Car. *Thrifty Rent-a-Car,* operating out of the Truckee Airport, rents cars and four-wheel-drives, with snow tires, chains and ski-racks; call (916) 587-2588 or (916) 546-2334 for information. Other car rental agencies in the area include *Avis* (702) 831-5494, *Budget* (702) 831-6483, *Compacts Only* (702) 831-3726, and *National Car Rental System* (916) 587-6748.

If you are driving in the area in wintertime, a word of advice: "winterize" your car; always carry tire-chains, and use them when the conditions so require; DO NOT park on any public street, or in any other "snow-plow" area — it's against the law; watch out for ice, especially black ice; and generally, exercise due caution, and take extra care when driving in winter conditions.

SEASONAL EVENTS. January. During the last week of the month, the Incline Village community celebrates *Winterskol,* a week-long winter carnival; several ski races are held at the Ski Incline area.

February. Locally sponsored *Sierra Sweepstakes Sled Dog Races* are held at the Truckee Airport, lasting two whole days. Some 75 teams compete in three-dog and eight-dog freight categories for a $5,000 purse. Contact the Truckee-Donner Chamber of Commerce on (916) 587-2757 for more information.

March. North Tahoe's biggest winter carnival, *Snowfest,* provides for ten whole days of fun and excitement. Most of the region's ski areas participate, and events include celebrity and other ski races, fireworks at Tahoe City, a torchlight parade at Squaw Valley, the crowning of a Snowfest Queen, and several other gala happenings. The festival is usually scheduled to begin on the first Saturday of the month.

June. Held at the Truckee Airport on the last weekend of the month each year, the *Truckee Airshow* features several air events, including aerobatics and "historic war games." Also, earlier in the month the annual *Lake Tahoe Classic Boat Race* gets underway, spanning four days; the highlight of this Classic is its 89-statute-mile race.

July. The entire North Tahoe area comes alive on the Fourth, with firework displays over the lake, off the shores of Tahoe City, Kings Beach and Incline Village. Later, in the month the *Sand Harbor Music Festival* comes to Sand Harbor (just south of Incline Village), bringing several talented musicians and hundreds of enthused fans to the sandy beach.

August. Again, Sand Harbor hosts a bonanza of *Shakespeare* performances, featuring a cast that's made up of members of professional theater companies. And at the Truckee River Park in Truckee, the annual *Rodeo* provides for a weekend of wild fun. Also during the month, the *Antique Boat Show* draws boat enthusiasts to the Tahoe Boat Company Marina at Tahoe City; restored precious wooden boats are featured. Of interest, too, is the annual *Tevis Cup Race* — a 100-mile one-day horse race that starts at Squaw Valley and finishes at Auburn.

The *Greater North Lake Tahoe Chamber of Commerce* and *Convention Bureau* publish an annual "Calendar of Events," available free from their office at the Lighthouse Center; or call (916) 583-2371.

TOURS. Foremost among North Lake Tahoe's tour operators is *See Tahoe Tours* (702) 832-0713, which offers tours of Lake Tahoe, Carson City and historic Virginia City, featuring live commentary and complimentary breakfast and lunch. Other tour operators in the area include *Safari and Tours* (702) 831-4657, and the Tahoe City based *Roundabout Tours* (916) 583-6677 who offer around-the-lake tours on board a London double-decker bus. Tours of North Tahoe's *Historic Homes* are also offered by the North Lake Tahoe Historical Society; call 583-1762 for reservations and information.

Air Tours. For sightseeing flights from Tahoe-Truckee Airport contact *Coyote Flying Services* (916) 587-6914, or *Sierra-Tahoe Aviation* (916) 587-4433; and for scenic glider rides call *Donner Aviation* on (916) 587-6702. Also the *Cal-Vada Seaplane Base* at Homewood, 6 miles south of Tahoe City, offers some exciting aerial sightseeing possibilities on board Super Cub seaplanes; phone (916) 525-7143.

PLACES OF INTEREST. Truckee. Located at intersection of I-80 and Highways 89 and 267. This is an historic, 1860's railroad town, with a wealth of restored 19th century buildings. In downtown visit the *Truckee Hotel, I.O.O.F. Hall, Oak & Brass Shoppe, Southern Pacific Depot, Loading Dock, Truckee Jail House, Gray's Log Cabin, Alpenglow Store, C.B. White's, La Vieille Maison, Star Hotel, Chinese Herb Shop*, and *Rocking Stone Tower* where a 17-ton boulder balances on a natural pedestal. See *Truckee* section earlier in this book for map and details.

Donner Memorial State Park and Museum. 4 miles west of Truckee on Donner Pass Road; (916) 587-3841. Several short walks lead to the campsites of the ill-fated Donner Party families, who spent the 1846-47 winter here. Also seen here is the *Emigrant Monument,* built on the site of the Breen family cabin. Nearby is Donner Lake, offering boating opportunities, and the *Emigrant Museum* where artifacts from the Central Pacific Railroad days can be viewed, as well as picture slide shows and old photographs recounting the Donner Party ordeal. The museum is open daily, 10-12 and 1-4; admission 50¢.

Western America Ski Sport Museum. Near Boreal Ridge exit off I-80. View ski exhibits dating from 1860; Snowshoe Thompson history and artifacts. Also some Squaw Valley Winter Olympic Games memorabilia. Open May-Oct., Wed.-Fri., 12-4, Sat. and Sun. 11-5, closed Mon.; admission free. (916) 426-3313

Squaw Valley. 6 miles northwest of Tahoe City, off Hwy 89. This is the site of the 1960 Winter Olympic Games; old ski jump can still be seen. Also ride the *Squaw Valley Aerial Tram* to the Granite Chief restaurant perched at 8200 feet; lovely scenery enroute. Aerial tram operates June 30-Sept. 2, 10-5.

Fanny Bridge and Outlet Gates. Located at the Tahoe City Y (intersection of Hwys 89 and 28). The bridge is a summertime favorite; watch Rainbow trout in pool beneath the bridge. The dam at the Outlet Gates was built in 1910. This is also the lake's sole outlet.

Gatekeeper's Cabin. Just south of Outlet Gates, reached via a small side road off West Lake Blvd. (between Truckee River Bank and Bridgetender restaurant). Restored log cabin situated in park-like setting, now a museum operated by North Lake Tahoe Historical Society. View artifacts and old Tahoe photographs. Open May-Oct., 11-5.

Watson's Log Cabin. In the heart of Tahoe City, on North Lake Blvd. Oldest building in the area, built in 1880's as the honeymoon cottage of Robert and Stella Watson. Now houses *Potter's Wheel*, a Navajo rug and pottery store; some Indian baskets. Open business hours.

Roundhouse Mall. In Tahoe City. Restored 1890's Southern Pacific Railroad building, now housing gift shops and one or two restaurants. At the front of the mall is the *Tahoe Boat Company Marina*, where some antique boats can be viewed during the annual Antique Boat Show. Nearby, in the *Boatworks Mall* visit two or three art galleries. Malls open at 10 a.m.

Cobblestone Mall. In Tahoe City, off North Lake Blvd. A charming replica of a Bavarian Alpine Village; some worthwhile gift shops and a cafe. Open-ended mall.

Fleur du Lac. 4 miles south of Tahoe City on Hwy 89. This is the former Henry J. Kaiser Estate, where "Godfather II" was filmed. Great big stone wall encircles the estate, and it is not open to public. It is best viewed from the lake; take a cruise on board North Lake Tahoe Cruises' *Sunrunner*, for this pauses before the estate, with commentary on its history.

Cal-Vada Seaplane Base. In Homewood, off Hwy 89. Seaplane rides for aerial sightseeing. Open summer.

Chamber's Landing. Just past Homewood, reached via a small side road off Hwy 89. Here is a fabulous 1870's over-water clubhouse, perched on an odd-shaped pier, now operating as cocktail bar and lounge; great views of the lake. Also there is a sandy beach here. The clubhouse is open during summer.

Sugar Pine Point State Park. Nearly 8 miles south of Tahoe City. 2000-acre park with several enchanting walks through it. Visit the fabulous *Ehrman Mansion*, located at the end of a small side road, east off the highway (the turnoff is marked with a "picnic area" sign). The mansion is a magnificent, gabled and turreted three-story edifice, built in 1903 and billed as "the finest High Sierra summer home in California." Several interesting outbuildings are seen here as well, including a water tower, and power generating plant, and on the grounds is an ancient 1860's cabin, *General Phipps' Cabin*. The grounds are quite splendid, offering picnicking possibilities, and can be toured more or less year-round. The mansion is open in the summer months, with State Park personnel conducting tours through it. State Park fee is $2.00 per car.

D.L. Bliss State Park. Just south of Sugar Pine Point, Hwy 89. A 957-acre park, with some wooded walks and one or two sandy beaches. Several interesting rock formations to be seen here, quite at random; especially interesting is the *Balancing Rock*, located just inside the park. Also visit the *Old Lighthouse* site above *Rubicon Point* (the deepest point on Lake Tahoe's shoreline, with a 1400-foot vertical drop). Open May through September.

Emerald Bay State Park - Vikingsholm. See South Lake Tahoe *Places of Interest* section.

Kellogg Mansion. In Tahoe Vista, Hwy 28. Built around 1910 as the summer home of the cereal king from Battle Creek, this now houses a French-seafood restaurant, *La Playa*. Lovely use of native stone.

Northstar. Just over the Brockway Summit (north of Kings Beach), off

Hwy 267. A 2500-acre "model development," dating from the early 1970's. There is a ski area and golf course worth visiting here.

Stateline Fire Lookout. Located above Crystal Bay, near the Cal-Nev Stateline. Take the street between the Nevada Lodge and Tahoe Mariner casinos, turn right at the fire station, then continue straight down, bearing left all the way until you reach a dirt road turnoff with a wooden gate; the Lookout is a short way down the dirt road. Visit inside the Forest Service Lookout, and enjoy some spectacular views of the lake and Sierras; some picnicking possibilities. Open during the summer months; dirt road is impassable in snow season.

Ponderosa Ranch. Situated at the southeast corner of Incline Village, off Hwy 28. A rambling western theme park, where the TV series "Bonanza" was filmed. The park provides for family entertainment, especially enjoyable to children. Visit the *Cartwright Home, Mystery Mine Shaft, Ponderosa Church,* petting farm, and several western shops and museums with interesting displays of ancient firearms, carriages, wagons, and farm machinery. Also visit stables for scenic horseback rides through the Ponderosa back country. Open May-Oct., 10-6; admission $5.00 adults, $4.00 children. For information, call (702) 831-0691.

Sand Harbor Recreation Area. 2 miles south of the Ponderosa Ranch, off Hwy 28. A lovely sand beach, with picnic area; one or two enclosed swimming areas. July through Sept., a Shakespeare festival and some live music can be enjoyed here. Open May-Oct.

Spooner Lake State Park. Some worthwhile walks, and a lake. Look for turnoff off Hwy 28, just before Spooner Junction (intersection of Hwys 28 and 50).

Art Galleries. *Timberline Crafts Gallery,* 590 Lakeshore Drive, Incline Village (702) 831-2460; pottery, stained glass, blown glass, jewelry and weavings. *Lake Gallery* at Boatworks Mall, Tahoe City (916) 583-1002 and Raley's Center, Incline Village (702) 831-4544; fine prints of works by internationally famous artists. *Spectrum Gallery,* Boatworks Mall, Tahoe City (916) 583-0801; artists of national repute represented. *Sierra Galleries,* Boatworks Mall, Tahoe City; bronze sculptures and paintings. *High Sierra Silver Works,* 600 N. Lake Blvd., Tahoe City (916) 583-1600; a variety of artists, material and media, with an operating jewelry studio. *The Potlatch,* 324 Ski Way, Incline Village (702) 831-2485; Indian jewelry, wood carvings, stone carvings and western art. *Crystal Visions,* Roundhouse Mall, Tahoe City (916) 583-2539; stained glass, ceramics and pottery, some watercolors. *Lakeside Gallery,* 8636 N. Lake Blvd., Kings Beach (916) 546-3135; oils by local artists. *Noah's Gallery,* 8645 N. Lake Blvd., Kings Beach (916) 546-3513; oils and acrylics.

NEARBY ATTRACTIONS. Reno. This is in many ways the "Las Vegas of Northern Nevada," located some 35 miles northeast of Lake Tahoe and reached via I-80 or Highway 395. It has a population of roughly 100,000, and professes to be "The Biggest Little City in the World." It boasts a wealth of casinos, hotels and restaurants — some 20,000 hotel rooms and over 300 restaurants — with live entertainment to be found at several. Of particular interest here is *Bally's* (formerly *MGM Grand Hotel*) where some fabulous shows can be enjoyed, including "Hello Hollywood Hello" in which a real live DC-9 appears on the stage; Bally's also boasts one of the largest casinos in the world, the size of two football fields. Worth visiting too is the *Harrah's Automobile Collection* where, on a 10-acre site, more than one thousand antique cars, some of them truly classics, are on display — everything from Bugattis to Model A's to Deusenbergs, Pierce Arrows and Franklins; among these is John Wayne's Cadillac convertible, and the 1929 Deusenberg Dual Cowl Phaeton and 1930

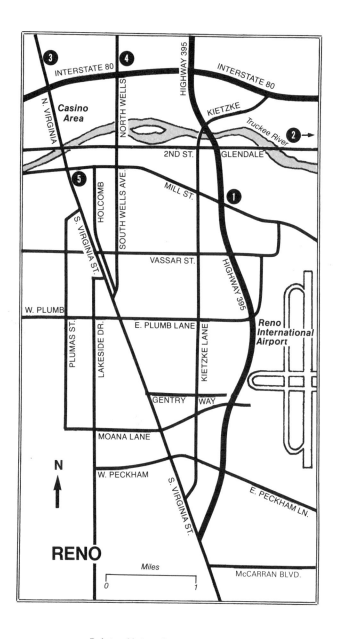

Points of Interest –
1) Bally's Grand Hotel
2) Harrah's Automobile Collection
3) University of Nevada
4) Washoe County Fairgrounds
5) Pioneer Theatre Auditorium

DuPont Royal Town Car, both of which featured as Daddy Warbucks' personal vehicles in the movie "Annie." Another point of interest is the *Harrold's Gun Collection* which features several antique guns, including Wild Bill Hickcock's .32 Smith and Wesson and a .45 Colt that once belonged to the legendary Jesse James. Take the time also to visit the *Pioneer Theatre Auditorium*, situated on Virginia Street just south of the casinos, quite distinctive with its gold geodesic dome; it was built in 1967 at an estimated cost of $2.5 million, and can accommodate up to 1,400 people. One or two spectator events worthy of mention here are the annual *Reno National Championship Air Races and Air Show*, the world's most daring and thrilling motorsports race, and the *Reno Rodeo*, one of the most colorful in the country. The air races are held in mid-September, and the rodeo in June. Following the air races shortly is the *Great Reno Balloon Race*, a memorable visual experience. Reno also has a university of considerable interest, which dates from 1864. For more information on Reno contact the *Reno-Tahoe Visitors Center* on 135 N. Sierra St., (702) 348-7788; or the *Reno-Sparks Chamber of Commerce*, 133 N. Sierra St., (702) 329-3558.

Virginia City. Billed as "the liveliest ghost town in the world," Virginia City is much to be recommended as a side trip. It is roughly 30 miles to the east of Lake Tahoe's Incline Village, reached by taking the Mount Rose Highway (Rt. 431) to the intersection of Hwy 395, then Rt. 341 over the Geiger Grade to Virginia City. Once a bustling, thriving metropolis of 30,000, and the largest city between San Francisco and St. Louis, Missouri, Virginia City now has a population of only 900. Yet nearly 500,000 tourists visit here every year. Tours of ancient silver mines, train rides on the Virginia & Truckee Railroad engines, and visits to the many splendorous Victorian mansions, notable among which are the *Savage* and *Mackay* mansions, are all worthwhile tourist activities. The downtown has several 1860's saloons and antique shops of sorts, as well as covered wooden walkways, reminiscent of the Old West, when silver was king. There is a huge cematary worth seeing here too, and dozens of other old buildings and museums, with countless antique exhibits. In September, the annual *Camel Races* provide for some fun and games, with side attractions such as parachuting and mock battles between the Confederates and Yankees. The town also has an ancient newspaper, the "Territorial Enterprise," on which Mark Twain worked briefly in the 1860's. The *Virginia City Visitors Bureau* (702-847-0177) is located on C Street, open year-round; films of Virginia City's bonanza days are shown at the center.

See also *Nearby Attractions* in the South Lake Tahoe section.

LAKE CRUISES. North Tahoe's only commercial cruise boat, the *Sunrunner*, is operated by *North Tahoe Cruises* from the Tahoe Boat Company Marina out front of the Roundhouse Mall in Tahoe City. Daily scenic and historic cruises of the west shore are offered from May through October; the itinerary includes the former Henry J. Kaiser Estate, "Fleur du Lac," where the movie "Godfather II" was filmed on location. Tour cost: $10.00 adults, $4.00 children. Also private charters for weddings, parties, conventions and other occasions are available. For reservations and information, call (916) 583-0141.

Other smaller charter vessels are available at many of the area's marinas.

RAFTING. Each year, river rafting gains in popularity at North Tahoe; tens of thousands of visitors to the area make it their favorite summertime recreation. The 4-mile section between Tahoe City and the River Ranch is particularly well-liked, with bushes, sand bars, marshes, one or two deep pools, and even a small section or two of mild rapids to be encountered along the way. Currently there are two commercial rafting companies operating on the Truckee River — *Mountain Air Sports* (916) 583-5606 and *Truckee River Raft Rentals* (916) 583-9724, both situated just to the west of the Tahoe City Y, on River Road (Hwy. 89). Raft rental cost is around $15.00 per person, and return rides to the point of origin are offered on board the rafting companies' shuttle buses.

Sections of the Truckee River north of the River Ranch, some of which provide excellent whitewater, can be enjoyed on private rafts.

 FISHING. Fish are plentiful in the North Lake Tahoe waters — Kokanee, lake trout, Mackinaw, Rainbow, Lahontan, Cutthroat, Brown and Golden. But you must possess, or obtain, a California or Nevada fishing license, and be wary of certain legalities and illegalities: for instance, do not exceed the catch limit of five game fish, five salmon, five trout, and five whitefish; do not spearfish or use live bait other than game fish taken from the lake; and do not fish within 200 yards of the mouth of any tributary to or from the lake. For more information on fishing in Lake Tahoe, obtain a copy of the "Angler's Guide" booklet from the *California Department of Fish and Game*, Box 73, Tahoe City, (916) 583-3325; or from the *Nevada Department of Fish and Game*, Box 10678, Reno, Nevada, (702) 784-6214.

FISHING GUIDES. Year-round fishing charters and guide services are available at the following: *King Fish*, Tahoe City (916) 583-0350; *Mickey's Guide Service*, Tahoe City (916) 583-4602; *Hooker for Hire*, Tahoe City (916) 525-5654; *All Seasons Sport Fishing*, Hirschdale, (916) 587-6452.

FISHING HOT SPOTS. *Rubicon Bay and Meeks Bay.* ½ mile out from the shore. Kokanee salmon are plentiful in summer.

Chambers Run. Opposite Chambers Landing, just north from Sugar Pine Point. Deeplining at depths of 100-300 feet.

McKinney Bay. Out from the Homewood shoreline. Mackinaw and Browns abound.

Kaspian Area. Just north of Kaspian Beach. Deepline for Mackinaw trout.

Tahoe Tavern Hole. Opposite the Tahoe Tavern Properties, ½ mile south of the Tahoe City shoreline. Mackinaw are abundant.

Tahoe Flats. 1½ miles out from the Lake Tahoe Dam at Tahoe City. Excellent trolling at depths of 25-30 feet.

Agate Bay. Out from the Tahoe Vista and Kings Beach shorelines. The entire bay is favored for deepline fishing at depths of 100-200 feet.

Stateline Point. Just beneath the peninsular tract of Crystal Bay. Deepline.

Crystal Bay. Along the Incline Village shoreline, not too far out from the shore. Topline is suggested for Rainbows and Browns.

Sand Harbor. South from Incline Village. Inshore fishing is excellent along rocky points.

Secret Harbor. 4 miles south of Sand Harbor. Trolling at depths of 20-70 feet, close to the shore.

Truckee River. Almost the entire river provides for excellent fly fishing.

 HIKING. Hiking is almost as keenly pursued in the North Tahoe area as it is on the south shore. Rangers from both the D.L. Bliss State Park (916-525-7277) and Sugar Pine Point State Park (916-525-7982) conduct guided hikes in the summer, usually on Saturday mornings. And then there are the dozen or so hiking trails snaking through surrounding areas, including the Granite Chief Area, the Lake Tahoe State Park (Nevada) area, and the west shore area. Permits are required in several of the areas, and such permits, as well as additional information, are available at these National Forest Service offices: *Truckee Ranger District,* Truckee (916) 587-3558; *Big Bend Ranger Station,* Soda Springs (916) 426-3609; *Foresthill Ranger District,* Foresthill (916) 367-2224.

HIKING TRAILS. Some of the trails are deep inside National Forest land, the trailheads approachable only by jeep or four-wheel-drive; these include, among others, the *Bear Trap Trail* in Antone Meadows, the *Sawmill Flat Trail* in the vicinity of Brockway Summit, and a variety of trails in the *Blackwood Canyon* area and the northwest section of the *Tahoe National Forest.* For information on these lesser known hiking areas, and for topographical maps, contact the Forest Service.

The following, however, are some of the better known and more popular trails:

West Shore Area. *Meeks Bay Trail.* Across from the Meeks Bay Resort, a dirt road leads to the trailhead, which is situated some 1½ miles southwest of the resort; this is a popular entry point into the Desolation Wilderness area. The trail winds south through the wilderness, past a series of little lakes — including Genevieve Lake, Crag Lake, Shadow Lake, Stony Ridge Lake and Rubicon Lake. 4.6 miles of trail; expect to use a whole day.

Sugar Pine Point Nature Trail. A 1½ mile loop, the trail starts out from near the Ehrman Mansion in the Sugar Pine Point State Park, then winds through the Sugar Pine Point Natural Preserve. Takes approximately 1 hour.

General Creek Trail. This is a particularly enchanting trail that begins by the General Creek Campground parking area, west of Highway 89, and wanders alongside of the General Creek, tracing a loop. Stream crossings and wooded picnic areas are encountered along the way, and some idyllic scenery. The loop is 5½ miles, expected to take 5 hours.

General Phipps Cabin Trail. The trail begins by the Sugar Pine Point picnic area, just off Highway 89, and leads to the site of the Indian fighter, General Phipps' cabin. It's a ½ mile trail, expected to take 30 minutes.

Twin Peaks Trail. Look for the trailhead on Ward Creek Boulevard, at the back of Pineland. The trail follows Ward Creek much of the way, ending at Twin Peaks; the summit offers a spectacular view of Lake Tahoe. Allow a full day for this 5-mile trail.

Paige Meadows Trail. Same trailhead as for the Twin Peaks Trail. This short, steep trail leads to the Paige Meadows, where a variety of wildflowers can be observed. 1 mile, 1 hour each way.

Five Lakes Trail. The trailhead is situated on the right side of Alpine Meadows Road, past Deer Park Drive, some 2 miles in from Highway 89. The trail is moderately steep, and leads to a group of five tiny lakes. 2 miles, 2½ hours each way.

Lake Tahoe State Park Area. *Tunnel Creek Station Trail.* The trailhead is located opposite Hidden Beach (a mile south of Ponderosa Ranch), just off Highway 28. A 1½-mile trail leads to the ruins of the old Tunnel Creek Station; views enroute are breathtaking. Duration of round trip approximately 4 hours.

Twin Lakes Trail. The trail begins opposite Hidden Beach, and snakes southeast to two tiny, adjoining lakes. It's a 5-mile round trip.

Spooner Lake Trail. Also from the Hidden Beach trailhead; this trail heads south, 16 miles, to Spooner Lake. The length of the trail warrants a pick-up at the Spooner Lake end.

North Canyon Trail. Parking is off the highway, adjacent to Spooner Lake. The trail winds north from the lake, through North Canyon, to Marlette Lake — a lake of moderate size that, during the 19th century, provided water for the V-flumes carrying logs down into Carson Valley. 10 miles of trail, which the beauty of North Canyon makes worthwhile; expect to use a full day.

Granite Chief Area. Situated northwest of Squaw Valley, this 40,000-acre backcountry recreation area boasts a bonanza of hiking trails; the area has been set aside exclusively for hikers and horseback riders. Contact U.S. Forest Service for information on the area's trails.

BICYCLING. A fun way to explore the North Tahoe area is on a bicycle (at least in summer). There are more than 50 miles of bike trails, the favorite stretch being the section along the Truckee River, northwest from Tahoe City. Bike-paths can also be found on the west shore, alongside of the highway, and on parts of the north shore.

Bike Rentals. There are several bike rental outlets catering to the needs of bike enthusiasts, among them: *Basecamp,* Tahoe City (916) 583-9530; *Olympic Bike Shop,* Tahoe City (916) 583-6415; and *Kings Beach Bicycles,* Kings Beach (916) 546-3664.

BEACHES AND PICNIC AREAS. North Lake Tahoe beaches offer a variety that ranges from sandy to pebbly to grassy — just take your pick. Picnic areas and restroom facilities are to be found on nearly all of them, and parking is available at several.

Sugar Pine Point State Park. Off Highway 89, just north of Meeks Bay. Facilities include picnic area, restrooms, pier, swimming, water ski area, boat docking and parking; a nominal parking fee is charged per car.

Kaspian Picnic Area and Beach. Off Highway 89, 3 miles south of Tahoe City. Picnic area, swimming, fire pits, and parking are available.

William Kent Beach. Just off Highway 89, 2 miles south of Tahoe City. Picnic area, swimming, lifeguard, fire pits, and restroom facilities; limited parking.

Tahoe City Commons Beach. In the heart of Tahoe City, just past the fire station. Picnic area, swimming, lifeguard, fire pits, grass area, volleyball courts, restrooms, and limited parking.

Tahoe Recreation Area Beach. Off Highway 28, ½ mile northeast of Tahoe City. Picnic area, swimming, fire pits, restrooms.

Lake Forest Beach. 1½ miles northeast of Tahoe City, at the foot of Tamarack Street (off Lake Forest Road). Picnic area, boat ramp, volleyball courts, swimming, fire pits, restrooms, and limited parking.

Patton Beach. Off Highway 28, just north of Carnelian Bay. Picnic area; and parking.

Agatam Beach. Also off Highway 28, in Tahoe Vista. Picnic area, restrooms; and parking.

Moondunes Beach. At the bottom of National Avenue (off Highway 28) in Tahoe Vista. A sandy beach, with excellent swimming facilities.

Secline Beach. In Kings Beach, at the foot of Secline Street. Parking is available off Highway 28.

Kings Beach Recreation Area. At the foot of Coon Street, in downtown Kings Beach. Picnic area is at the eastern end of the beach; restrooms, a boat ramp, volleyball courts and parking, too, are available.

Hidden Beach. 2 miles south from the Ponderosa Ranch, just off Highway 28. Offers swimming and hiking.

Nevada State Park at Sand Harbor. 4 miles south of Incline Village (or 2 miles south of Hidden Beach), just off Highway 28. Restrooms, boat ramp, swimming, lifeguard, and parking; a nominal fee is charged for parking.

CAMPING OUT. Campsites are available in nearly a dozen locations in the North Lake Tahoe area. Most of the camps are well managed and have restroom facilities, swimming, fishing, hiking and even riding.

Campgrounds. *Meeks Bay Resort.* On Highway 89, 10 miles south of Tahoe City. 28 sites, rental cabins, restrooms, store, boat ramp, swimming, no pets. No day limit. Reservations (916) 525-7242.

D.L. Bliss Campground. See *Campgrounds* in South Lake Tahoe section.

General Creek Campground. On Highway 89, 9 miles south of Tahoe City. 175 sites, restrooms, showers, swimming, hiking, riding, and fishing; 10-day limit. Open year-round. Reservations (916) 525-7982.

Kaspian Recreation Area Campground. On Highway 89, 3 miles south of Tahoe City. 10 sites, restrooms, swimming, hiking; 7-day limit. Phone (916) 544-6420.

William Kent Campground. Just off Highway 89, 2 miles south of Tahoe City. 95 sites, restrooms, beach, swimming, fishing; 7-day limit. Phone (916) 544-6420.

Tahoe State Recreation Area. On Highway 28, just north of Tahoe City. 39 sites, restrooms, showers, and fishing; 10-day limit. Reservations (916) 583-3074.

Lake Forest Campground. On Highway 28, 1½ miles northeast of Tahoe City. 21 sites, restrooms, showers, boat ramp, beach, swimming, fishing and hiking; no pets. 14-day limit. Phone (916) 583-5544.

Silver Creek Campground. On Highway 89 (on the Truckee River), 7 miles north of Tahoe City. 30 sites, restrooms, swimming, fishing, hiking and riding; 14-day limit. Phone (916) 587-3558.

Goose Meadows Campground. On Highway 89 (on the Truckee River), 9 miles north of Tahoe City. 30 sites, restrooms, swimming, fishing, hiking; 14-day limit. Phone (916) 587-3558.

Granite Flat Campground. On Highway 89 (on the river), 2 miles south of Truckee. 75 sites, restrooms, swimming, fishing, and hiking; 14-day limit. Phone (916) 587-3558.

Donner Memorial Campground. 2 miles west of Truckee, off Donner Pass Road in the Donner Memorial State Park. 125 sites, restrooms, showers, boat ramp, swimming, fishing, hiking and riding; 10-day limit. Reservations (916) 587-3841.

BOATING. During the summer the North Lake Tahoe witnesses an influx of water activity, much of it centered around the area's dozen or so marinas and public launching ramps. Many of the marinas offer everything from rentals and sales of boats, jet-skis, water-skis and sailboards, to repair service and even winter storage. Some even sport restaurants, snack bars and cocktail lounges.

Meeks Bay Marina. 10 miles south of Tahoe City, off Highway 89. Slips, boat ramp, gas supplies, rentals, snack bar. Launching fee: $5.00 in, $5.00 out. Open through summer. Phone (916) 525-7242.

High & Dry Marina. Off Highway 89, 6 miles south of Tahoe City. Buoys, forklift launching, gas supplies, repairs, rentals, sales and storage. Launching fee: $12.00 in, $12.00 out. Open summers. Phone (916) 525-5966.

Obexer's Marina. Off Highway 89, in Homewood. Slips, buoys, boat ramp, gas supplies, repairs, rentals, storage, snack bar. Launching fee: $5.00 in, $5.00 out. Open year-round. Phone (916) 525-7962.

Sunnyside Resort and Marina. 1½ miles south of Tahoe City, off Highway 89. Slips, buoys, forklift, hoist, gas supplies, repairs, rentals, storage and restaurant. Open through summer. Phone (916) 583-9420.

Tahoe Boat Company Marina. In Tahoe City, at the front of the Roundhouse Mall. Slips, buoys, gas supplies, repairs, rentals, sales, storage, snack bar. Launching fee: $25.00 one way, $40.00 in and out. Open through summer. Phone (916) 583-5567.

Sierra Boat Company. Off Highway 28, 1½ miles south of Kings Beach. Slips, buoys, gas supplies, repairs, rentals, storage. Launching fee: $20.00 one way. Open year-round. Phone (916) 546-2552.

Tahoe Vista Marina. Off Highway 28, Tahoe Vista. Slips, buoys, gas supplies, restaurant, and cocktail lounge; no launches. Open summers. Phone (916) 546-3185.

North Tahoe Marina. Also off Highway 28, next to the Tahoe Vista Marina. Slips, buoys, hoist, boat ramp, gas supplies, repairs, rentals, sales, storage, snack bar. Launching fee: $15.00 one way. Open through summer. Phone (916) 546-8248.

Public Launching Ramps are available at *Lake Forest* (1 mile north of Tahoe City), *Coon Street* (Kings Beach) and *Sand Harbor* (3½ miles south of Incline Village).

GOLF. North Lake Tahoe has seven golf courses, some with driving ranges and a couple of mini golf courses; following is a list of these:

Incline Executive Golf Course. Off Wilson Way in Incline Village. 18 holes, 3440 yards, 58 Par; green fee: $30.00/with cart (cart mandatory). A pro shop and a snack bar are available on the premises. For enquiries, call (702) 832-1150.

Incline Championship Golf Course. On Fairway Boulevard in Incline Village, just off Northwood Boulevard. 18 holes, 7120 yards, 72 Par; green fee: $50.00/with cart (cart mandatory). Facilities: pro shop, driving range, bar and snack bar. Enquiries: (702) 832-1144.

Woodvista Golf and Country Club. Wedged between Highways 28 and 267 in Kings Beach. 9 holes, 3100 yards, 35 Par; green fee: $12.00/9 holes, $18.00/18 holes. Carts, pro shop, driving range, and restaurant. Enquiries (916) 546-9909.

Tahoe City Golf Course. In Tahoe City, behind the Bank of America. 9 holes, 2700 yards, 33 Par; green fee: $10.00/9 holes, $15.00/18 holes. Carts, pro shop, driving range, restaurant. Enquiries (916) 583-1516.

Northstar-at-Tahoe Golf Course. Off Highway 267, 6 miles north of Kings Beach. 18 holes, 6897 yards, 72 Par; green fee: $24.00/all day, $14.00/twilight. Carts, pro shop, driving range, restaurant. Enquiries (916) 587-0290.

Ponderosa Golf Course. On Highway 267, 1 mile south of Truckee. 9 holes, 3000 yards, 36 Par; green fee: $17.00/all day. Carts, pro shop, snack bar. Enquiries (916) 587-3501.

Tahoe Donner Golf and Country Club. On Northwoods Boulevard, 2 miles west of Truckee. 18 holes, 7000 yards, 72 Par; green fee: $30.00/weekday, $40.00/weekend, $15.00/twilight. Carts, pro shop, driving range, restaurant and bar. Enquiries (916) 587-9440.

Miniature Golf Courses. *Magic Carpet Miniature Golf*. On Highway 28 in Carnelian Bay. Two courses available, one 19 holes and the other 28 holes. Phone (916) 546-4267.

Boberg's Mini-Golf. On Highway 28 in Kings Beach. Two 19-hole courses. Phone (916) 546-3196.

TENNIS. Tennis is popular in summer. And while several excellent courts are available at local private clubs, many of North Tahoe's schools and parks open up their courts to the public as well.

Tennis Courts. *Sugar Pine Point State Park.* Just off Highway 89, 8½ miles south of Tahoe City. 1 court; no lights.

Kilner Park. 2 miles south of Tahoe City, off Highway 89. 2 courts; lights. Phone (916) 583-5544.

Granlibakken. Just south of Tahoe City, at the end of Tonopah Drive (off Highway 89). 8 courts; no lights. Private lessons. Phone (916) 583-4242.

Squaw Valley Tennis Club. In Squaw Valley, at the end of Squaw Valley Road (off Highway 89). 4 courts; no lights. Private lessons. Phone (916) 583-0035.

Tahoe Lake School. On Grove Street in Tahoe City. 2 courts; lights.

North Tahoe High School. Just north of Tahoe City, on Polaris Road in Highlands. 4 courts; lights.

North Tahoe Regional Park. In Tahoe Vista, at the end of National Avenue. 5 courts; lights. Phone (916) 546-7248.

Kings Beach Elementary School. In Kings Beach, between Wolf Street and Steelhead Avenue. 2 courts; no lights.

Incline High School. On Village Boulevard in Incline Village. 4 courts; no lights.

Lakeside Tennis Club. In Incline Village, just off Highway 28. 13 courts; no lights. Private lessons. Phone (702) 831-5258.

HORSEBACK RIDING. With five fully stocked stables, and a variety of trail rides, scenic rides and breakfast, lunch and sunset rides in the offing, horseback riding has become a prime indulgence in the North Lake Tahoe area. And to cater to this indulgence, there's a stable in close proximity to wherever at North Tahoe you might be.

Area Stables. *Alpine Meadows Stables,* 4 miles north of Tahoe City, off Highway 89, (916) 583-3905; *Squaw Valley Riding Stables,* Squaw Valley Road, (916) 583-0419; *Tahoe Donner Equestrian,* at the Tahoe Donner Resort in Truckee, (916) 587-9809; *Northstar Stables,* at the Northstar Resort on Highway 267, (916) 562-1230; *Ponderosa Ranch,* on Highway 28 at the southeast corner of Incline Village, (702) 831-2154.

WINTER SPORTS. A renowned mecca of skiing, Lake Tahoe boasts 18 alpine ski areas, 163 ski lifts, and 11 nordic areas — and of those, 14 slopes, 116 lifts, and some 7 cross-country ski areas are concentrated in the North Lake Tahoe region. Among the downhill areas are the world-famous Squaw Valley and the equally renowned Alpine Meadows and Northstar-at-Tahoe, three of Tahoe's "Big Five" ski areas (the other two being Heavenly and Kirkwood). Among North Tahoe's cross-country areas is Royal Gorge, with a 3200-acre spread.

But skiing is not all that North Tahoe has to offer in winter; snowmobiling, tobogganing, sledding, and sleigh rides are just as popular.

Downhill Skiing. Most up-to-date information on ski areas and skiing conditions can be found in any one of several local periodicals, including the *Ski Tahoe* guide, available at several outlets, and the *North Tahoe Week,* also widely distributed in the area. For radio ski reports, tune in to any of the local stations — KOWL-AM1490, KZFR-FM103, KLKT-FM100, KRLT-FM94, KTHO-AM590.

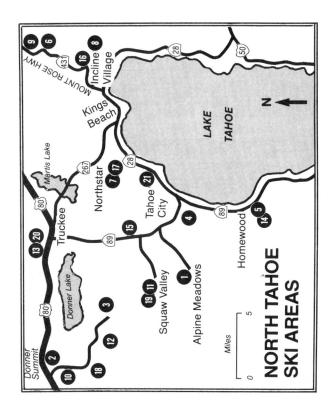

NORTH TAHOE SKI AREAS

Downhill Ski Areas –
1) Alpine Meadows
2) Boreal Ridge
3) Donner Ski Ranch
4) Granlibakken
5) Homewood Ski
6) Mount Rose
7) Northstar-at-Tahoe
8) Ski Incline
9) Slide Mountain
10) Soda Springs
11) Squaw Valley U.S.A.
12) Sugar Bowl
13) Tahoe Donner
14) Tahoe Ski Bowl

Nordic Ski Areas –
15) Big Chief Guides
16) Incline Cross-Country Center
17) Northstar Nordic Center
18) Royal Gorge
19) Squaw Valley Nordic
20) Tahoe Donner Nordic Center
21) Tahoe Nordic

The following are North Tahoe's downhill ski areas:

Alpine Meadows. 7 miles northwest of Tahoe City, at the end of Alpine Meadows Road (off Highway 89). Elevations: top 8700 feet, base 6840 feet; vertical drop 1730 feet. Facilities: 13 lifts, NASTAR races, lessons, rentals, child care, snack bar, restaurant, bar, and suttle bus. Lift prices: $27.00/adults, $11.00/children; half day: $18.00/adults, $8.00/children. Phone (916) 583-4232.

Boreal Ridge. 10 miles west of Truckee, just off I-80 (take Castle Peak exit). Elevations: top 7800 feet, base 7200 feet, vertical drop 600 feet. Facilities: 9 lifts, night skiing, lessons, rentals, snack bar and restaurant. Lift prices: $19.00/adults, $11.00 children; half day: $13.00 adults, $9.00/children. Phone (916) 426-3666.

Donner Ski Ranch. West of Truckee; take Soda Springs exit off I-80, then 3½ miles down old Highway 40. Elevations: top 7960 feet, base 7135 feet, vertical drop 825 feet. Facilities: 6 lifts, night skiing, lessons, rentals, snack bar and restaurant. Lift prices: $18.00/adults, $9.00 children; half day: $12.00/adults, $8.00 children. Phone (916) 426-3635.

Granlibakken. Just south of Tahoe City, at the end of Tonopah Drive (off Highway 89). Elevations: top 6610 feet, base 6330 feet, vertical drop 280 feet. Facilities: 2 lifts, lessons, rentals, snack bar. Lift prices: $10.00 adults, $6.00/children; half day: $6.00/adults, $4.00/children. Phone (916) 583-4242.

Homewood. On Highway 89, 6 miles south of Tahoe City. Elevations: top 7880 feet, base 6230 feet, vertical drop 1650 feet. Facilities: 10 lifts, lessons, rentals, restaurant and snack bar. Lift prices: $18.00/adults, $5.00/children; half day: $14.00/adults, $3.00/children. Phone (916) 525-7256.

Mount Rose. 10 miles north of Incline Village, on Mount Rose Highway (Route 431). Elevations: top 9700 feet, base 8250 feet, vertical drop 1450 feet. Facilities: 5 lifts, lessons, rentals, bar, snack bar and restaurant. Lift prices: $20.00/adults, $10/children; half day: $14.00/adults, $7.00/children. Phone (702) 849-0704.

Northstar-at-Tahoe. Just off Highway 267, 6½ miles southeast of Truckee. Elevations: top 8600 feet, base 6400 feet, vertical drop 2200 feet. Facilities: 9 lifts and 1 gondola, NASTAR races, lessons, rentals, day lodge, store, snack bar, restaurant, and shuttle bus. Lift prices $25.00/adults, $13.00/children; half day: $18.00/adults, $9.00/children. Phone (916) 562-1010.

Ski Incline. Ski Way, Incline Village. Elevations: top 7600 feet, base 6700 feet, vertical drop 900 feet. Facilities: 7 lifts, lessons, rentals, snack bar, restaurant. Lift prices: $20.00/adults, $14.00/children; half day: $14.00/adults, $11.00/children. Phone (702) 832-1122.

Slide Mountain. 11 miles north of Incline Village, on Mount Rose Highway (Route 431). Elevations: top 9700 feet, base 8200 feet, vertical drop 1500 feet. Facilities: 3 lifts, lessons, rentals, snack bar and restaurant. Lift prices: $17.00/adults, $11.00/children; half day: $12.00/adults, $8.00/children. Phone (702) 849-0303.

Soda Springs. West of Truckee; on old Highway 40, near Soda Springs exit off I-80. Elevations: top 7352 feet, base 6700 feet, vertical drop 652 feet. Facilities: 3 lifts, night skiing, snowboarding, lessons and rentals. Lift prices: $15.00/adults, $10.00/children; half day: $10.00/adults, $8.00/children. Phone (916) 426-3666.

Squaw Valley U.S.A. 8 miles northwest of Tahoe City,m at the end of Squaw Valley Road (off Highway 89). Elevations: top 8900 feet, base 6200 feet, vertical drop 2700 feet. Facilities: 27 lifts and 2 gondolas. NASTAR races, night skiing, lessons, rentals, snack bar, restaurants, and shuttle bus. Lift prices: $28.00/adults, $5.00/children; half day: $20.00/adults, $5.00/children. Phone (916) 583-6985.

Sugar Bowl. West of Truckee, take Soda Springs exit off I-80, then onto old Highway 40. Elevations: top 8383 feet, base 6881 feet, vertical drop

1502 feet. Facilities: 10 lifts and 1 gondola, night skiing, lessons, rentals, snack bar and restaurant. Lift prices: $25.00/adults, $13.00/children; half day: $17.00/adults, $10.00/children. Phone (916) 426-3651.

Tahoe Donner. 2½ miles northwest of Truckee, off Donner Pass Road. Elevations: top 7350 feet, base 6750 feet, vertical drop 600 feet. Facilities: 3 lifts, lessons, rentals, snack bar and restaurant. Lift prices: $15.00/adults, $9.00/children; half day: $11.00/adults, $7.00/children. Phone (916) 587-6028.

Nordic Ski Areas. Several miles of marked and groomed trails are available at North Tahoe's nordic ski areas; lessons, maps, and equipment rentals are offered at all of these areas.

Big Chief. Located on Highway, 3 miles north of Squaw Valley. 40 miles of trails, day and moonlight tours, a restaurant, and child care facilities. Phone (916) 587-4723.

Clare Tappen Lodge. Old U.S. 40, Soda Springs. 21 miles of trails, lodge. Trail fee: $4.00. Phone (916) 426-3632.

Incline Cross-Country Center. Off Golfer's Pass Road, at the Incline Village Executive Golf Course. 10 miles of trails; tours, restaurant. Trail fee: $4.50/adults, $2.50/children. Phone (702) 831-5190.

Northstar Nordic Center. Off Highway 267, 6½ miles south of Truckee. 25 miles of trails; tours, lodge, restaurant, child care. Trail fee: $7.00/adults, $4.00/children. Phone (916) 562-1010.

Royal Gorge. A mile from I-80, at the Soda Springs exit. 153 miles of trails; tours, restaurant. Trail fee: $11.50/adults, $6.50/children. Phone (916) 426-3871.

Squaw Valley Nordic. Off Highway 89, 8 miles north of Tahoe City; near Squaw Valley Theater. 30 miles of trails, tours, restaurant, child care. Phone (916) 583-2746.

Tahoe Donner Nordic Center. West of Truckee; ½ mile from I-80, off old Highway 40. 30 miles of trails; tours, lodge. Trail fee: $9.00/adults, $5.00/children. Phone (916) 587-9821.

Tahoe Nordic. Off Highway 28, 2½ miles northeast of Tahoe City. 30 miles of trails; tours, day lodge. Trail fee: $5.00/adults, $3.00/children. Phone (916) 583-9858.

Wilderness Cross-Country Ski Areas. At least ten different cross-country ski areas are situated in State Parks or National Forest lands; following are some of the more popular ones:

Sugar Pine Point State Park. The trailhead is located at the State Park Ranger Station, just off Highway 89 (½ mile south of Tahoma).

Blackwood Creek. 2 miles south of Sunnyside, a forest service road branches off Highway 89 and leads to the trailhead, some 2½ miles in.

Paige Meadows. 2 miles south of Tahoe City; take Pine Avenue off Highway 89, then right into Tahoe Park Heights Drive, and left into Silvertip Drive. Follow Silvertip to the trailhead at the end of the street.

Pole Creek. 9 miles north of Tahoe City, off Highway 89; trailhead is located across the street from Big Chief Lodge.

Brockway Summit Area. The trailhead is located between Northstar and Kings Beach, off Highway 267.

Snowmobiling facilities are available at some of the area's golf courses. Apart from the courses, other North Tahoe tracts open to snowmobiles include the *Blackwood Creek Wilderness Area* (2 miles in from the Kaspian State Park Recreation Area), and the open meadow near the summit of *Mount Rose.*

Snowmobile Rentals are available at: *Snowmobile Connection*, Tahoe City (916) 583-1516, Tahoe Vista (916) 546-7248; *Snowmobiling Unlimited*,

Tahoe City (916) 583-5858; and *North Tahoe Sports Center*, Incline Village (702) 831-0472.

Snow Play Areas: *Granlibakken Ski Area*, ½ mile south of Tahoe City; *North Tahoe Regional Park*, at the end of National Avenue in Tahoe Vista; and *Northstar Area*, ½ mile south of Northstar Drive (off Highway 267).

ENTERTAINMENT. North Lake Tahoe's entertainment scene is as widely dispersed as the area. At the stateline in Crystal Bay, the *Tahoe Biltmore, Crystal Bay Club* and *Cal-Neva Lodge* feature live entertainment most nights. While in Incline Village, *Hyatt Lake Tahoe* draws some big names in entertainment to its *Sugar Pine Lounge*. For show information and reservations, call (702) 831-0660/Tahoe Biltmore, (702) 831-0512/Crystal Bay Club, (702) 832-4000/Cal-Neva Lodge, and (702) 831-1111/Hyatt.

Across much of the rest of the North Tahoe area, live music can be enjoyed at several different restaurants, bars and lounges, among them — the *Bar of America*, in downtown Truckee (916) 587-3110; *The Passage*, Commercial Row, Truckee (916) 587-7619; *Waterfront*, at the Lighthouse Center in Tahoe City (916) 583-5131; *Emma Murphy's*, in downtown Tahoe City (916) 583-6939; *Olympic Village Inn*, on Squaw Valley Road (916) 583-1501; *Carnelian House*, on the highway in Carnelian Bay (916) 546-5954; and *Schaffer's Mill*, in the Northstar Village off Highway 267, (916) 562-1015.

DINING OUT. Dining out in North Lake Tahoe is generally good to excellent in the better restaurants. Several of the oldest and best establishments in the area specialize in various European cuisines, although Oriental and Mexican restaurants can be just as easily found.

Restaurant prices — based on full course dinner, excluding drinks, tax and tips — are categorized as follows: *Deluxe*, over $25; *Expensive*, $15-$25; *Moderate*, $10-$15; *Inexpensive*, under $10.

Gourmet

The Pines. *Deluxe*. At Hyatt's Hotel-Casino, in Incline Village. Reservations (702) 831-1111.

Hugo's Rotisserie. *Expensive*. At the Hyatt, Incline Village. Roast duckling and lobster tails are among the favorites here. Reservations (702) 831-1111.

Christy Hill. *Expensive*. Off Squaw Valley Road in Squaw Valley . A long-standing Squaw Valley institution, open for breakfast, lunch and dinner. Mouth-watering homemade chocolate mousse pies. Reservations (916) 583-8551.

Pfeifer House. *Expensive*. Highway 89, ½ mile north of Tahoe City. Splendid European dishes and large portions; 30 entrees. Reservations (916) 583-3102.

Steaks and Seafood

Captain Jon's. *Deluxe*. At the Tahoe Vista Marina, in Tahoe Vista. Lakeside setting. Among the favorites are Poached Salmon and Roast Duck with Blueberry or Oyster sauce; also worthwhile are the seafood salads and fresh fruit daiquiries. Reservations (916) 546-4819.

Blue Water Sea Garden. *Expensive*. At the back of Country Club Mall, Incline Village. Reservations (702) 831-2086.

Schaffer's Mill. *Expensive*. At Northstar, off Highway 267. Lovely historic setting. Open breakfast, lunch and dinner during ski season. Phone (916) 562-1015.

Ric's. *Expensive*. Kiosk Mall (395 North Lake Blvd.) in Tahoe City. Phone (916) 583-1835.

Jake's on the Lake. *Expensive*. At the Boatworks Mall in Tahoe City. Sweeping views of the lake. Phone (916) 583-0188.

C.B. White's. *Expensive*. Commercial Row, Truckee. Beef Wellington is a favorite, encased in delicate pastry and topped with mushroom pate. Reservations (916) 587-4364.

Wolfdale's. *Expensive*. 640 N. Lake Tahoe Blvd., Tahoe City. Creative California seafood. Lake views. Reservations (916) 583-5700.

French

La Playa. *Deluxe*. Highway 28, Tahoe Vista. Creative French-country seafood. Housed in old Kellogg Mansion, with unobstructed lake views. Reservations (916) 546-5903.

Le Petit Pier. *Deluxe*. 7252 North Lake Blvd., in Tahoe Vista. Acknowledged as one of the finest French restaurants in California, and with a splendid lakefront setting. Specialties are lamb and pheasant dishes. Reservations (916) 546-4464.

La Chiminee. *Deluxe*. 8504 North Lake Blvd., Kings Beach. A unique dining experience in classic French cooking. Reservations (916) 546-4322.

Swiss

Tahoe House. *Expensive*. On Highway 89, ½ mile south of Tahoe City. Homemade pastas, and freshly baked bread and pastry desserts. Phone (916) 583-1377.

Alpenhaus. *Expensive*. Highway 89, Tahoma. Veal and filet specialties. Also all-you-can-eat Basque dinners on Thursday nights. Breakfast features freshly-baked muffins. Reservations (916) 525-5000.

Swiss Lakewood Lodge. *Expensive*. 5505 West Lake Boulevard, Homewood. Fine Swiss and Continental cuisine. Closed Monday. Reservations (916) 525-5211.

Italian

Bacchi's Inn. *Moderate*. On Lake Forest Road, just north of Tahoe City. Established in 1932, it has been owned and operated by the same family for three generations. Great family dinners and generous portions. Its Minestrone Soup is famous the world over, featured in several gourmet magazines. Reservations (916) 583-3324.

Azzara's. *Moderate*. At the Raley's Center in Incline Village. Phone (702) 831-0346.

Continental

River Ranch. *Expensive*. Highway 89, at Alpine Meadows. Historic lodge in a lovely on-the-river setting. Specialty Roast Duck Montmorency, and vintage wines by the glass. Reservations (916) 583-4264.
Wild Berries. *Deluxe*. At the back of Country Club Mall, Incline Village. Lamb and game specialties; creative desserts. Closed Monday. Reservations (702) 831-2000.

American

Col. Clair's. *Moderate*. North Lake Blvd., Tahoe Vista. Cajun and Creole specialties; homemade soups. Southern-style desserts. Reservations (916) 546-7358.
Quinn's Log Cabin Restaurant. *Inexpensive*. Stateline Road, Crystal Bay. Housed in a charming log cabin with stone fireplace; great burgers, soups and salads. Phone (916) 546-7529.

Mexican

Las Margaritas. *Moderate*. At the Christmas Tree Village, in Incline Village. Reservations (702) 831-3500.
Hacienda Del Lago. *Moderate*. Boatworks Mall, Tahoe City. Multi-flavored margueritas, and large deck overlooking the lake. Enormously popular. Phone (916) 583-0358.

Chinese

Water Wheel Restaurant. *Moderate*. 115 West Lake Blvd., Tahoe City. Phone (916) 583-4404.

PINE CONES

Silver Pine

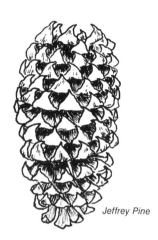

Jeffrey Pine

Sugar Pine

Yellow Pine

Lodgepole Pine

Whitebark Pine

Foxtail Pine

Pinyon Pine

122

LAKE TAHOE FISH

Lake Trout

Brook Trout

Brown Trout

Golden Trout

Rainbow Trout

Kokanee Salmon

Lahontan Cutthroat Trout

Mountain Whitefish

Paiute Cutthroat

123

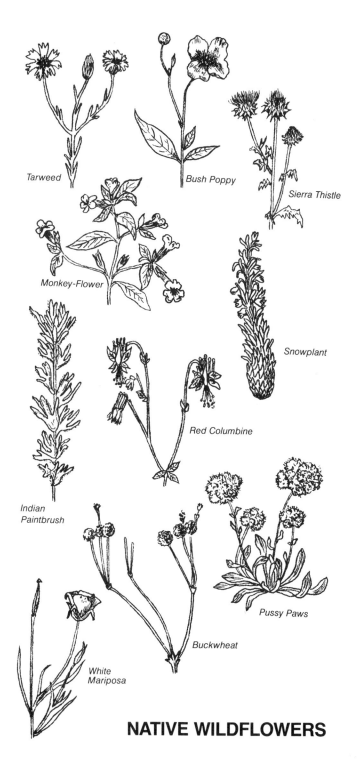

Tarweed

Bush Poppy

Sierra Thistle

Monkey-Flower

Snowplant

Indian
Paintbrush

Red Columbine

White
Mariposa

Buckwheat

Pussy Paws

NATIVE WILDFLOWERS

124

SIERRA WILDLIFE

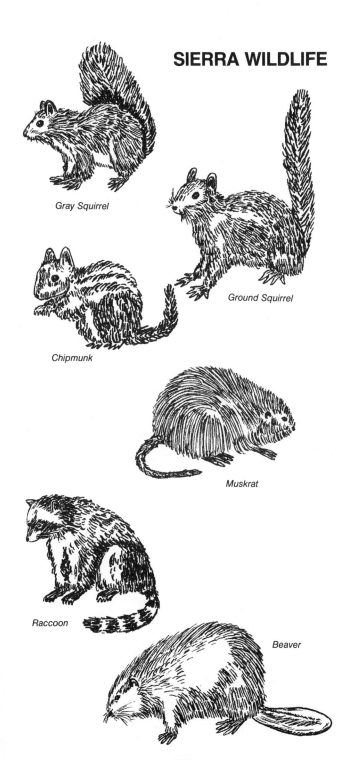

Gray Squirrel

Ground Squirrel

Chipmunk

Muskrat

Raccoon

Beaver

Coyote

Black Bear

Gray Fox

INDEX

The abbreviation SLT stands for South Lake Tahoe.
The abbreviation NLT stands for North Lake Tahoe.